Eye-Catching Crochet

Fashion Accessories You Can Make

Janet Rehfeldt

Martingale®
& COMPANY

Dedication

To my family and friends for their constant encouragement and help. To each and every one of you, you never fail to allow me to see my dreams.

Eye-Catching Crochet:
Fashion Accessories You Can Make
© 2006 by Janet Rehfeldt

Martingale®
& C O M P A N Y

Martingale & Company
20205 144th Avenue NE
Woodinville, WA 98072-8478 USA
www.martingale-pub.com

Library of Congress Cataloging-in-Publication Data
Library of Congress Control Number: 2006002328

ISBN-13: 978-1-56477-676-1
ISBN-10: 1-56477-676-X

Printed in China
11 10 09 08 07 06   8 7 6 5 4 3 2 1

Mission Statement

Dedicated to providing quality products and service to inspire creativity.

Credits

President ◆ Nancy J. Martin
CEO ◆ Daniel J. Martin
COO ◆ Tom Wierzbicki
Publisher ◆ Jane Hamada
Editorial Director ◆ Mary V. Green
Managing Editor ◆ Tina Cook
Technical Editor ◆ Donna Druchunas
Copy Editor ◆ Liz McGehee
Design Director ◆ Stan Green
Illustrator ◆ Laurel Strand
Cover Designer ◆ Stan Green
Text Designer ◆ Regina Girard
Photographer ◆ Brent Kane

Contents

Introduction

Browsing through fashion and gossip magazines, you see celebrities wearing crocheted chokers, bracelets, belts, scarves, and even gloves. Wandering through the fashion department in your favorite store, you see crochet accessories and accents on every rack. Yet even with this popularity, patterns for crocheted accessories are hard to find.

I wrote this book to fill that need. Working with novelty yarns and ribbons, along with beads and other materials, I wanted to design chic upscale accessories that would appeal to a wide range of crocheters. With projects ranging from hats, scarves, and gloves to jewelry, purses, and shawls, my goal was to create crocheted accessories that you can wear with pride.

The resulting collection will take you from play to work and even to the opera in style. Several patterns—such as the Crossed-Stitch Belt, Textured Watchband and Anklet, So Very Chic Headband, and Felted Mini Purse—include choices of different materials and fibers so you can create the look that suits your personal style.

But I didn't do this all on my own. I had the help of wonderful designers that I am happy be able to call my friends. So, with a little help from my friends, I have come up with crocheted accessories that I just know you'll find not only beautiful but also stylish. Wearing your own crocheted accessories will make you feel like a fashion diva.

The patterns in this book are designed for the crocheter with knowledge and experience of the basic crochet stitches. In order to pack as many patterns as possible into a limited amount of space, I have not included illustrations or instructions for the basic crochet stitches such as slip stitch, single, half double, or double crochet. If you're unfamiliar with any of the stitches used in this book, I suggest you pull out your favorite crochet reference guide to help you along in creating your accessories. I hope that you have as much fun creating your accessories as all of us had in putting this book together for you.

—*Janet Rehfeldt*

Terrific Tools

It doesn't take any special tools or gadgets to crochet accessories. Some yarn, a hook, a few stitch markers, a pair of scissors, and you're on your way. However, there are some great tools and gadgets on the market that can be helpful and fun to use.

- *Crochet hooks* vary in size from one manufacturer to the next. The hook sizes given in the materials section of each pattern are listed in both U.S. and metric sizes; for example, size J-10 (10.0 mm). Check your hooks for the metric size before beginning your pattern. Gauge checks, available at local yarn shops, allow you to check the size of unmarked hooks.

- *Stitch markers* are useful for marking increases, decreases, and the beginning of rounds (see "Working with Stitch Markers" on page 14).

- *Row counters* come in handy for tracking the rows on stitch-pattern repeats and the number of times you need to increase or decrease in a pattern.

- A good pair of small *scissors* is always needed for cutting yarn ends. If you tend to misplace your scissors, a thread-cutter pendant is just the ticket. It's also perfect for travel.

- A good *tape measure* with both inches and metric measurements is a must for taking accurate measurements and checking your gauge.

- Large, *blunt-end needles* are necessary for weaving in ends and sewing seams. The needles with a curved tip are wonderful for getting into and under the strands of the stitches.

- Big-eye or split-shaft *beading needles* make it easier to thread beads onto yarn or thread. The needle eye is split down the center so you can put your yarn or thread through. You can also use a dental floss threader with a loop to thread beads onto yarn or thread.

Choosing Yarns

The yarns used in this book have been given standard-weight symbols so you can substitute other yarns. For example, many companies create railroad-track ribbon yarn. As long as the weight and yardage are very close to the yarn used in the pattern, you should have no trouble substituting a similar product from another manufacturer. In several designs, we've made versions using different materials so you can see how easy it is to change the look of an item simply by changing the yarn or thread. (See "Crocheting with Leather" on page 8 and "Crocheting with Wire" on page 9 for sizing information on these materials.)

If the yarn has a dye lot, make sure you purchase enough yarn to finish your project. Read the yarn label for fiber content and follow the laundering instructions listed on the yarn label to make sure your items have a wonderfully long life.

Yarn Conversion Chart
m = yds x 0.9144
yds = m x 1.0936
g = oz x 28.35
oz = g x 0.0352

Novelty Yarns

Many wonderful yarns and threads on the market today are perfect for crocheting accessories. The different types of novelty fibers—such as eyelash, smooth and textured ribbons, linen, alpaca, leather, fur, faux fur, and carry-along yarns with bits of sequin or fluff—make for a wonderland of colors and textures.

Standard Yarn Weights						
Yarn-Weight Symbol and Category Names	1 SUPER FINE	2 FINE	3 LIGHT	4 MEDIUM	5 BULKY	6 SUPER BULKY
Types of Yarns in Category	Sock, Fingering, Baby	Sport, Baby	DK, Light Worsted	Worsted, Afghan, Aran	Chunky, Craft, Rug	Bulky, Roving
Crochet Gauge Ranges in Single Crochet to 4"	21 to 32 sts	16 to 20 sts	12 to 17 sts	11 to 14 sts	8 to 11 sts	5 to 9 sts
Recommended Hook in Metric-Size Range	2.25 to 3.5 mm	3.5 to 4.5 mm	4.5 to 5.5 mm	5.5 to 6.5 mm	6.5 to 9 mm	9 mm and larger
Recommended Hook in U.S.-Size Range	B-1 to E-4	E-4 to 7	7 to I-9	I-9 to K-10.5	K-10.5 to M-13	M-13 and larger

Accessories provide a great way to try out new yarns because, in many cases, they're small enough to be made or embellished with just one ball. Check your local yarn shop's sale bin for odd-lot balls of great yarns for experimenting.

Ribbons

Crocheting with ribbon is no different than crocheting with yarn; you work your stitches in the same manner. Some ribbons are slippery. Placing the balls into plastic baggies while working helps keep the ribbon from tangling as you crochet.

Railroad-track or railroad-tie ribbon yarns have sections that are empty in the center. Be sure that you're picking up the entire strand of ribbon and not just one of the threads along the side edges as you crochet with these yarns.

Carry-Along Yarns

A carry-along yarn is normally a thin core of thread with novelty ribbon, fluff, beads, sequin, or eyelash interspersed along its length. It is carried along with a strand of regular yarn and the two strands are crocheted together as one. If a little bit of ribbon, fluff, beads, sequin, or eyelash comes up just when you work a yarn over to create a loop or finish your stitch, try to hook the strand just beyond the bit of novelty. Doing so may create a loop, but it will allow the little novelty bits to show nicely on your piece, which is what they're supposed to do.

Eyelash Yarns

Thin eyelash yarns are usually made of a core thread with short, medium, long, or even multiple-length strands, referred to as eyelash, interspersed and twisted into the core. To crochet with this type of eyelash, carry it along with another thread or yarn. Try to keep the strands of eyelash to the right side of the crochet by wrapping the yarn over the hook just ahead or behind the eyelash strand and pushing the eyelash to the right side as you work. Sometimes the strands will gravitate toward the wrong side of the work or get caught in the stitches. If this happens, use a blunt tapestry needle or a knitting needle to pull the strands out and to the right side.

Thick eyelash yarns are normally worked alone. These yarns are best suited for working with a larger hook and open stitches. The texture of the stitches can make it difficult to see where to put your hook. The best thing to do when you can't find the opening of the stitches is to go by feel, using your fingers to lift or open the stitches. Don't worry if you're slightly off on the placement of your stitch; the nature of the yarn covers most mistakes.

Slubbed Yarns

Yarns with slubs are similar to carry-along yarns in that the slub can sometimes come up just when you're working a yarn over to create a loop or finish your stitch. When this happens, try to hook the strand just beyond the slub. This will create a loop, but it's OK. Just remember that loops contribute to the texture slubbed yarns are meant to produce.

Hemp, Jute, and Gimp Cording

Working with cording is almost the same as working with crochet cotton. Hemp, jute, and gimp cords are available in bead shops and in the jewelry or beading section of local craft shops.

*When you want a firm texture,
try crocheting with hemp or jute cording.*

Ripping Back or Unraveling

No one likes to have to rip back or unravel their work. But sometimes you absolutely must unravel a mistake. When working with smooth yarns, this goes quickly. But if you're working with angora, mohair, eyelash, or slub yarns, go very slowly, teasing the yarn by working the strand back and forth from side to side at each stitch. The little hairs in angora and mohair as well as the slubs, eyelashes, and sequin bits on novelty yarns often get caught and crocheted into other stitches. You don't want to break or tear the yarn or your stitches as you rip.

Crocheting with leather may be a little more awkward than working with traditional yarn or thread; however, as long as you use the right type of leather lacing with the right size hook, you can create truly one-of-a-kind, trendy accessories, such as belts, chokers, bracelets, headbands, and watchbands.

Flat Leather Lacing

Flat leather lacing is stiff and is best suited for belts. Use lacing that is between 3/32" and 1/8" (2.5 to 3 mm) wide. You can use larger stripping or lacing for things such as rugs or chair mats, but it can be too hard to work with when making accessories.

The key to crocheting with leather lacing is to use simple crochet stitches and the right size hook. Using

a hook that is too small will be an exercise in futility. When working with leather, I hold my hook in the knife manner rather than the pencil manner. Using your thumb to push the leather on and off the hook can also be helpful.

See "Resources" on page 76 for mail-order suppliers of flat leather lacing.

Suede Lacing

Suede lacing isn't quite as stiff as flat leather; however, you should stick to lacing that is between 3/32" and 1/8" (2.5 to 3 mm) wide if you can find it. Be careful not to buy the thick type of suede stripping or lacing that is common in craft shops. Although it may be approximately 1/8" (3 mm) wide, it's also about the same in thickness (or height), making it too difficult to crochet with. The flatter the suede lacing, the easier it is to work with.

See "Resources" on page 76 for mail-order suppliers of suede lacing.

Round Leather Lacing

Round lacing is the easiest to crochet with. This type of lacing is used for jewelry making, in addition to the normal leather craft uses. Lacing that is 1/32" to 1/16" (1 to 2 mm) in diameter is available in most craft and bead shops and through mail order. I enjoy using this type of leather lacing best because I can work with smaller hooks and more complicated stitches than I can with the flat, wider lacings. The 1/32" (1 mm) lacing is perfect for wrist and ankle bracelets, chokers, watchbands, and headbands, while the 1/16" (2 mm) lacing is great for belts and headbands.

Leather Jewelry Cord

Leather jewelry cord comes in various thicknesses, normally between 1/64" and 1/8" (0.5 mm and 3 mm), but it can be found in even heavier thicknesses. It is stiffer than leather lacing but comes in a wider variety of colors. You will find leather jewelry cord in bead shops and in the beading section of most craft shops.

Crocheting with Wire

Working with wire is nothing like working with thread, yarn, leather, or most any other medium. Wire doesn't behave like a flexible fiber. It molds to the hook and holds the shape you create as you pull the strand of wire up with your hook. You won't get the flowing texture that you get with fibers and it can be difficult to see the stitches in the finished item especially when using fine-gauge wire. However, you can create stunning pieces of jewelry, as well as headbands and belts, using wire. The results are well worth the effort.

The size, or diameter, of wire is listed in gauge. The higher the number, the finer the wire. When you first begin, using fine wire from 28 to 32 gauge (0.33 to 0.2 mm) makes it easier to learn how to manipulate the wire than using heavier wire.

If your wire comes in a coil, carefully uncoil five yards or so, then secure one end around the coil. If you leave the coil unsecured, the wire will tangle and wrap itself into a large mess that can be difficult to recover. If your wire comes on a spool, unwrap five or so yards, then secure the wire into the slit at the top of the spool. If there is no slit, make a slit or tape the wire to the top of the spool. When you need additional wire, unwind another five or so yards and resecure.

Crochet your stitches the same as you would with yarn or leather, but each time you yarn over your hook and bring the loop or strand of wire through the stitch or loop you're working, push the shank of the crochet hook up into the new stitch to open it up and use your fingers to shape the work. Try to make the final loop of each stitch the same size. This will help you find the top of each stitch on subsequent rows or rounds.

Ripping back mistakes can be difficult, but it's not impossible. Use your hook to unwork each loop and strand of the stitch. Straighten the wire by running it through your fingers or fingernails to get as many kinks out of the wire as possible. Don't yank or pull hard on the wire or it will break.

To add beads to crocheted wire, follow the same instructions that appear on page 10 for working with fiber. See "Resources" on page 76 for suppliers of craft wire.

Crocheting with Beads

Crocheting beads into a project is a great way to add spice or elegance. You can change the look of an accessory, taking it from simple to spectacular just by adding a few beads.

Stringing the Beads

If your beads come strung on a hank rather than loose, carefully hold the string over a shallow dish with your fingers about 2" above the knot. You need to be able to knot the string around the yarn you're using for your project, so you may need to drop several beads if the strand is tightly strung. Holding the strand over a shallow dish, cut the string just above the knot, allowing any loose beads below your fingers to fall into the dish. Tie the strand onto the project yarn or thread with as small a knot as possible. Push the beads slowly down onto the project yarn or thread. Don't push from the top of the bead strand. Work with just a few beads at a time or the strand may break. Using a needle that fits through the bead, thread the empty bead strand through the needle, then pick up and string any loose beads onto the project yarn or thread.

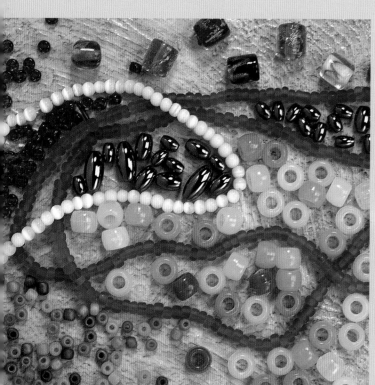

Most beads are sold loose by the ounce or in packages. There are several methods for getting loose beads onto yarn or thread.

You can use a big-eye or split-shaft needle to thread (or string) the beads onto the yarn or thread you're using. Open the needle at the center and insert your project yarn or thread into the "big eye." Spill the loose beads into a shallow dish and scoop the beads onto the needle, then push them onto the project thread or yarn.

If you don't have a split-shaft beading needle, you can use a dental floss threader that has a loop at one end of it to string the beads. Insert the thread or yarn into the loop, then place or scoop the beads onto the shaft of the floss threader, and push the beads onto the project thread or yarn.

For yarns and threads that are too thick to pull through beads with beading needles or dental floss threaders, such as hemp or jute cord, place a small amount of glue about 1" along the end of your project yarn or thread, remove the excess, and allow it to dry; then place or scoop the beads onto the solid tip with the dried glue and slide them down onto the yarn or thread.

When working with leather lacing, make sure the beads fit over the lacing you're using. As long as you can thread the leather lacing through the beads, you can work with it. You can use the strand of leather as your threading tool for stringing the beads onto the leather.

When working with wire, string beads directly onto the wire.

Working Crochet Stitches with Beads

Crocheting a bead into the piece using a single crochet allows the bead to sit slightly above the stitches on the finished piece. The bead will slant slightly to the right or left of the stitch.

Bead Single Crochet (bsc) on a Wrong-Side Row

The easiest way to crochet with beads is to make sure you're working on a wrong-side row so that the beads pop automatically to the right side of the work.

Insert the hook into the next stitch and bring a bead up to the hook (see fig. 1), keeping the bead at the back of the work, yarn over and pull the strand through the stitch (see fig. 2), yarn over and pull the strand through two loops on the hook (see fig. 3).

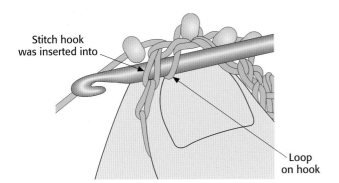

Stitch hook was inserted into

Loop on hook

Fig. 1

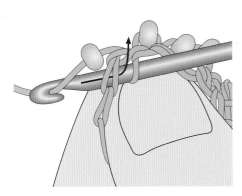

Fig. 2

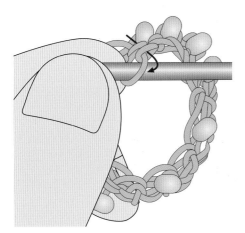

Fig. 3

Bead Single Crochet (bsc) on a Right-Side Row

There are times when you'll need to add your beads while crocheting on the right side of the work. To do this, bring the yarn and bead forward before working the stitch.

Bring the yarn to the front of the work, insert hook into next stitch, bring the bead up close to the work, yarn over, pull through the stitch (see fig. 4), yarn over, pull through two loops on hook.

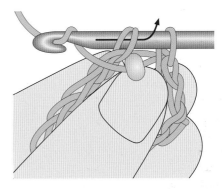

Fig. 4

Bead Slip Stitch (bead sl st)

Insert hook into next stitch, bring bead up to work, yarn over, pull bead and strand through stitch.

Don't Overload
Be sure not to string more than 150 to 200 beads at a time, because the beads can shred the yarn or thread being used for your project. Push the beads well down onto the yarn or thread into groups of about 10 beads, with long gaps between groups so that you don't have to constantly push the beads down as you work.

Felting

What is felting? Basically, felt is matted wool. Anyone who has accidentally shrunk her favorite wool sweater beyond rescue—when it mistakenly was added to the washer—so that it now fits an 18" doll has felted. The process that created the now shrunken, matted, miniature version of your sweater can be intentionally applied to wool fiber to make sturdy items such as hats, mittens, booties, slippers, vests, jackets, and so forth.

Wool fibers are covered by layers of scales that overlap each other. When the wool is placed into hot water, the scales open up, and agitating the item causes the scales of the wool to adhere and mat or "felt" together. Rinsing the item in cold water closes the scales and stops the felting process.

Superwash wools won't felt, as they have been treated to guard against shrinkage. Wools with more than 10% of another fiber may not give you the desired shrinkage. You can, however, crochet novelty fibers, such as eyelash or metallic threads, along with a strand of wool yarn in your piece and still felt for a unique texture, such as in the Felted Mini Purse on page 70.

Felting by Machine

Set your washer to a hot wash, a low water level, and a heavy-duty agitation cycle. You may need to add about 1 or 2 cups of boiling water if your hot-water heater is set at a lower temperature for child safety. Add about ½ to 1 tablespoon (7.5 to 15 ml) of baby shampoo, wool-wash soap, or other mild soap to the water. Allow the item to agitate.

Using heavy rubber gloves to prevent burning your hands, check your item after about five minutes. Continue to agitate, checking every three to five minutes until the item appears to be the size that you want. Reset the agitation cycle as needed until you have the desired size. Do not leave the washer while felting. Once your item starts to felt, it will shrink quickly.

When you're happy with the size of the item, set your machine to rinse with cool or cold water and rinse the item. Don't allow your item to go through an entire spin cycle. Once the washer sounds like all the water has drained, stop the spin cycle. If you allow the item to go through the entire spin cycle, it may put permanent creases into your item.

> **NOTE:** Front-loading machines may not work, since you need to be able to stop and start the agitation process as well as open the washer to check your projects. If using a front-loading machine, be sure the water level is low enough before opening the washer so that it does not flood your laundry room.

Tips for Successful Felting

Remember that no matter what wool you're using, you must have a nice, loose gauge. If your gauge is looser than the gauge stated in the instructions, it's fine; however, if your work is tighter, you need to either go up in hook size or crochet more loosely. You won't get a good felt if your stitches are tight.

When beginning to felt by machine, if you have a hot-water tap close to your washing machine, turn the hot water on and let it run to get nice and hot before you start the washing machine. Then when you start the washing machine, the water should be hot as it starts to fill, rather than cold turning hot.

If you place your items into a zippered pillowcase, it will keep lint from clogging your washer. If your drainage hose goes into a sink you have easy access to, you can place the foot section of a pair of panty hose over the end of the drainage hose and secure it with a rubber band to catch the lint from the wool.

Special Instructions and Stitches

Some of the patterns in this book will require that your gauge match what is listed in the pattern in order for your accessory to fit correctly or turn out like the one on the model. And some patterns use stitches other than the basic crochet stitches, such as Rose Garden Shoulder Shawl or Reversible Ripple Scarf. The following section explains the special instructions and stitches used in the patterns.

Calculating Your Gauge

Gauge refers to the number of stitches and rows you have, while tension refers to how tightly or loosely you hold your yarn while working.

For most of the patterns in this book, it doesn't matter if your gauge is exactly on target. However, for those patterns that do require the gauge to be met so that the item comes out the correct size, it's important to take the time to make a small gauge swatch.

Make the required number of chains in the stitch technique used in the pattern to get 20 stitches. If your pattern is single crochet, you would make 21 chains; half double crochet, 22 chains; and so forth. Work the pattern for 20 rows. Measure the width of the swatch. Divide the 20 stitches by the width measurement for the number of stitches per inch. Measure the length of the swatch. Divide the 20 rows by the length measurement for the number of rows per inch.

For example:

1. Swatch measures 5¾" wide.
2. 20 stitches divided by 5.75 equals 3.47 stitches per inch. (Round off to 3.5 stitches per inch.)
3. Swatch measures 5" long.
4. 20 rows divided by 5 equals 4 rows per inch.

If you have more stitches per inch than are listed in the pattern, go up in hook size. If you have fewer stitches per inch, go down in hook size. If your stitches match but your rows are slightly off, it's usually a matter of correcting your tension. If you have fewer rows than listed in the pattern, tighten up your tension, which is controlled by the way you hold the ball yarn through your fingers. If you have more rows, loosen up a bit by easing up on the way you're holding the ball yarn through your fingers.

On projects that are worked in the round, you may find that your gauge will be slightly different than working back and forth. It's advisable to make your swatch in the round.

> **NOTE:** For small items, working a gauge swatch 10 stitches by 10 rows is sufficient.

Sewing an End-to-End or Finished-Edge Seam

When working on a finished edge, where you see the top chain of the work, work the seam back and forth from one edge to the other, inserting the needle under the top chain of the stitch on one edge, then under the top chain of the stitch on the opposite edge (see fig. 5). Pull the threads up snugly after every five or six stitches. Don't pull the threads too tight or the piece will pucker.

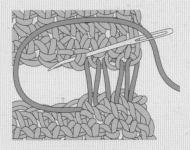

Fig. 5

Working in the Bottom Hump of the Chain

Working in the bottom hump of the chain gives you a beautiful finish. It also makes picking up the stitches much easier and cleaner when you need to add ribbing or attach one piece to another piece. Chain the number listed in the pattern, turn the chain over, and insert the hook into the bottom hump of the chain (see fig. 6). The pattern instructions will tell you when you should use this technique.

Fig. 6

Changing Colors

To change colors, drop the old color to the wrong side, then work the last two loops off the hook with the new color (see fig. 7).

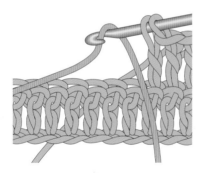

Fig. 7

Working with Multiple Colors

Do not cut the yarn unless stated in the instructions. Carry the unused color on the wrong side. In some cases, you will just allow it to form a loose strand along the back of the work. In other cases, you will actually drop the old color and carry it up along the side edge of the work for several rows or rounds. In this case, bring the old-color yarn strand up to the next row and crochet around the unused strand of yarn while working the first stitch of the row or round, securing the strand so that it does not form a large, loose loop on the edge of the work.

> **NOTE:** *Don't use the old color to work the first stitch. You're only looping around the old yarn color with the current yarn color to keep it neat and tidy along the edge until you need to work with it again. Don't pull the old color tight or it will pucker the edge of the work.*

Working with Stitch Markers

Crochet markers need to be open-ring markers that you can insert under the loops of the stitches. As you come to the markers, you remove the marker, work your stitch or stitches, then reinsert the marker where instructed. The pattern instructions will tell you to place a marker (pm) in a specific stitch to mark the beginning of a round or areas to increase or decrease.

For marking the beginning of rounds, you need to move the marker up at the beginning of each new round.

For increasing and decreasing, the pattern will instruct you to work up to a specific number of stitches before or at the marker. For example, if an instruction reads "Sc to 3 sts before marker," locate the marker and then count back three stitches, excluding the stitch with the marker (see fig. 8).

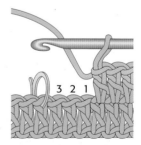

Fig. 8

Increasing and Decreasing

To increase, work two stitches into the same stitch. There are several different types of decreases, depending on which crochet stitch you're working.

Single Crochet Decrease (sc2tog)

This decrease is worked over two stitches. Insert hook into the next stitch, yarn over, pull through the stitch, insert hook into the next stitch, yarn over, pull through the stitch, yarn over, pull through all three loops on hook.

Half Double Crochet Decrease (hdc2tog)

This decrease is also worked over two stitches. Yarn over, insert hook into the next stitch, yarn over, pull through the stitch, insert hook into next stitch, yarn over, pull through the stitch, yarn over, pull through all four loops on hook.

Double Crochet Decrease (dc2tog)

This double decrease is worked over two stitches. Yarn over, insert hook into the next stitch, yarn over, pull through the stitch, yarn over, pull through two loops on hook, yarn over, insert hook into the next stitch, yarn over, pull through the stitch, yarn over, pull through two loops on hook, yarn over, pull through all three loops on hook.

Working with a Double-Ended Crochet Hook

Working with a double-ended crochet hook, also called a double-ended afghan hook, allows you to create reversible textures and color patterns. You normally use two contrasting or coordinating colors or textures of yarn. The Reversible Ripple Scarf on page 42 uses this method of crochet.

With color A, work your chain to the number specified in the pattern. Insert hook into the second chain from the hook, yarn over, pull a loop up onto the hook, *insert hook into next chain, yarn over, and pull a loop up onto the hook (see fig. 9). Repeat from * across the chain.

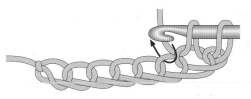

Fig. 9

Push the work all the way down to the other end of the hook. Turn the work.

Make a slip knot with color B and place the loop on the hook, pull the loop through the first loop on the hook (see fig. 10); *yarn over, pull loop through the next two loops on the hook*; repeat from * to * across the loops on the hook (see fig. 11) until only one loop remains on the hook. Do not turn the work.

Fig. 10

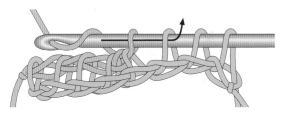

Fig. 11

Working into the Vertical Bars

The vertical bars of the stitch are the strands or bars that run up and down vertically. These are formed when you pull the loops up onto the hook (see fig. 9). The instructions will tell you whether to work under the bar or go between the bars.

Working into the Horizontal Stitches

The horizontal stitches (or bars) of the work are the top two chain loops of the stitch. These are formed when you yarn over and pull the loop (or strand) through the loops on the hook (see fig. 11). The instructions will indicate whether to work under just the top loop of the stitch, just the bottom loop of the stitch, or both loops. Insert your hook under the loop or loops of the stitch as specified in the pattern (see fig. 12).

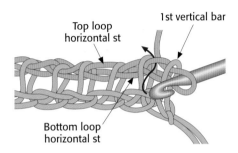

Fig. 12

With color B, chain 1, insert the hook under either the second vertical bar or whichever horizontal-stitch loops the pattern calls for (see fig. 12), yarn over, pull loop up onto the hook; *insert hook into next bar or loop as indicated, yarn over, pull loop up onto hook*; repeat from * to * across. Push the work down to the other end of the hook and turn the work.

With color A, yarn over, pull loop through the first loop on the hook; *yarn over, pull through the next two loops on the hook*; repeat from * to * across the loops on the hook until only one loop remains on the hook. Do not turn the work (see fig. 12).

Continue to work in this manner, pulling up the loops onto the hook and then working the loops off the hook.

When to Turn and Change Colors

On the first few rows, you may have trouble remembering when to turn the work and when not to turn the work as well as when to change yarns and when not to change yarns.

- When all the loops are on the hook, turn the work.
- If there is only one loop left on the hook, do not turn the work.
- When all the loops are on the hook, change yarn color.
- If there is only one loop left on the hook, do not change yarn color.

NOTE: *Because you're working with more than one skein of yarn, the skeins can become tangled when you turn your work. To keep the yarns from tangling, turn the work from right to left first, then next time, turn from left to right.*

Crossed Stitches

Crossed stitches are worked by skipping a stitch, working a single, half double, or double crochet into the next stitch, then working a single, half double, or double crochet stitch into the stitch that was skipped (see fig. 13). Some crossed stitches may have you skip a stitch, work a double crochet in the next stitch, then a chain stitch, then work a double crochet in the skipped stitch.

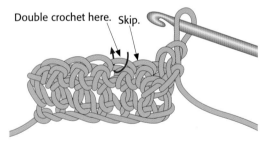

Fig. 13

Extended Single Crochet (esc)

Insert hook into the stitch, yarn over, pull up a loop, yarn over, pull through one loop on hook (see fig. 14), yarn over, pull through two loops on hook (see fig. 15).

Fig. 14

Fig. 15

Abbreviations

approx	approximately
beg	begin(ning)
bl	back loop
bsc	bead single crochet
CC	coordinating color
ch	chain
ch sp	chain space(s)
cl	cluster
cont	continue(ing)
dc	double crochet
dc2tog	double crochet 2 stitches together
dec	decrease(ing)
esc	extended single crochet
fl	front loop
hdc	half double crochet
hdc2tog	half double crochet 2 stitches together
inc	increase(ing)
lp(s)	loop(s)
m	meter(s)
MC	main color
mm	millimeter(s)

patt	pattern
pm	place marker
prev	previous
rem	remaining
rep	repeat(s)
rnd(s)	round(s)
RS	right side
rsc	reverse single crochet
sc	single crochet
sc2tog	single crochet 2 stitches together
sk	skip
sl st	slip stitch
sp	space(s)
st(s)	stitch(es)
tog	together
tr	triple crochet
WS	wrong side
yd(s)	yard(s)
yo	yarn over hook

Skill Levels

The following skill categories were developed by the Craft Yarn Council of America. In this book, each project is labeled with a skill level so that you can choose according to your abilities.

◼☐☐☐ **Beginner:** Projects that use only basic stitches. Minimal shaping.

◼◼☐☐ **Easy:** Projects that use yarn or thread with basic stitches, repetitive stitch patterns, simple color changes, shaping, and finishing.

◼◼◼☐ **Intermediate:** Projects that use a variety of techniques, such as basic lace patterns or color patterns, midlevel shaping, and finishing.

◼◼◼◼ **Experienced:** Projects with intricate stitch patterns, techniques, and dimension, such as nonrepeating patterns, multicolor techniques, detailed shaping, refined finishing, and the use of fine threads and small hooks.

Rose Garden Shoulder Shawl

By Janet Rehfeldt

Wearing this shawl reminds me of sitting in a beautifully peaceful rose garden. The carry-along yarn has little tufts of fringe that resemble scattered leaves lying throughout this elegant shawl. If you use a yarn other than ribbon, you will get a completely different gauge and look to your shawl.

Skill Level: Easy ◼◼◻◻

Approximate Dimensions

47" wide x 26" deep (excluding fringe)

Featured Stitches

Back loop (bl)
Chain (ch)
Extended single crochet (esc), page 16

Materials

A: 2 balls of Sevilla from Katia (100% nylon; 153 yds/140 m; 1.75 oz/50 g), color 35 **(4)**

B: 2 balls of Paradise from Plymouth Yarn (80% rayon, 20% nylon; 164 yds; 1.75 oz/50 g), color 31 **(2)**

Size K-10.5 (6.5 mm) crochet hook (or size required to obtain gauge)

Size F-5 (3.75 mm) crochet hook for adding fringe

Gauge

8 sts = 4" in esc using size K-10.5 (6.5 mm) crochet hook

> **NOTE:** *One strand each of A and B are held together throughout. Work first and last stitch through both loops; work all remaining stitches of row in the back loop only.*

Shawl

From each of A and B, cut 115 pieces of fringe 12" long for a total of 230 pieces; set aside.

Row 1: With size K-10.5 hook and 1 strand each of A and B held tog, ch 3, leaving a 7" tail, esc in 2nd ch from hook, 2 esc in last ch, turn. [3 esc]

Row 2 (inc row): Ch 2, esc in 2nd ch from hook, bl esc in each of next 3 esc, esc in first ch of beg ch-3 on prev row, turn. [5 esc]

Row 3 (inc row): Ch 2, esc in 2nd ch from hook, bl esc in each esc across, esc in first ch of beg ch-2 on prev row, turn. [7 esc]

Rows 4–47: Rep row 3, inc 1 st at beg and end of each row until you have 93 sts. Fasten off, leaving a 7" tail.

Fringe

Using size F-5 hook and 1 strand each of A and B held tog, fold fringe in half to form a lp. Beg at upper right corner, insert crochet hook from back to front, draw lp through, then bring ends through lp and tighten. Rep with rem strands, placing fringe approx ½" apart along side edges and placing 1 fringe in tip at bottom of shawl. Keep tails at beg and end of shawl as part of fringe. Trim fringe ends even when finished.

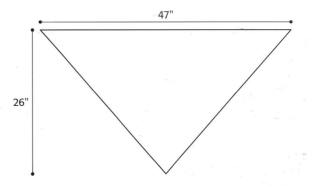

Sea Treasures Stole

By Hazel Carter

The seas contain countless treasures, many as yet unknown to us. This design focuses on shells, a favorite inspiration for artists and crafters for their pleasing shapes and colors. The stole is made in two parts, each starting from one of the ends. Each half consists of a scallop-shell edging, a section of open-shell pattern, and a sea-fan design for the center. The two latter designs are separated by a spacer band of double crochet, lace holes, and another row of double crochet. The halves are then joined by a crochet seam.

Skill Level: Intermediate ◼◼◼◻

Approximate Dimensions
24" wide x 90" long (after blocking)

Featured Stitches
Chain (ch)
Double crochet (dc)
Single crochet (sc)
Triple crochet (tr)

Materials
3 balls of Lace Mohair from Karabella Yarns (61% superkid mohair, 8% wool, 31% polyamid; 540 yds/500 m; 1.75 oz/50 g), color 165 🔢

Size F-5 (3.75 mm) crochet hook (or size required to obtain gauge)

OR

2 skeins of Merino Lace from Skacel (100% fine merino wool; 1375 yds; 100 g), color 729 🔢

Size G-6 (4 mm) hook (or size required to obtain gauge)

Gauge
15.75 dc = 4"

> **NOTE:** The scallop-shell edging is worked partly sideways and partly lengthwise, making it more elastic than with the conventional beginning chain. The remainder of the stole is worked lengthwise. Work loosely throughout.

Stole (First Half)

Scallop Shell Edging

Row 1: *Ch 4, dc in 4th ch from hook*, rep from * to * 3 more times, turn. [4 lps]

Row 2: Ch 1, sc in first ch-4 lp, ch 3, (sc, ch 5, sc) into 2nd ch-4 lp, ch 3, sc in 3d ch-4 lp, turn.

Row 3: Ch 2, sk first ch-3 sp, (1 tr, ch 2) 4 times into ch-5 sp, sk 1 sc and next ch-3 sp, sc in last sc, turn.

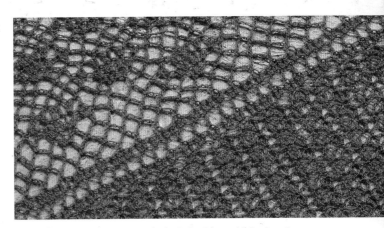

The Sea Treasures Stole knit in Skacel Merino Lace

Row 4: Ch 1, (3 sc in ch-2 sp, sc into tr) 4 times, 3 sc in last ch-2 sp, sc in empty ch-4 lp of first row to anchor, turn.

Row 5: Ch 1, sc in each sc of sp, (ch 3, sk sc made over tr, sc in each sc of sp) 4 times, sc into lp of first row.

This completes first scallop. Do not fasten off, rep rows 1–5 seven more times. [8 scallops]

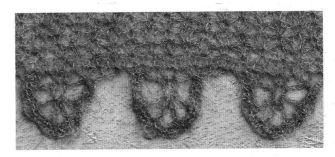

Open Shells

Work along straight edge of scallops and into the bottom of the ch-4 lps as follows:

Foundation row: Ch 3, dc into dc lp, *1 dc in sp between lps, 2 dc into dc lp*, rep from * to * as far as final lp, turn. [95 dc, including beg ch 3]

Row 1: Ch 1, sc in first dc, *ch 1, sk 1 dc, (dc, ch 1, dc) in next dc—shell worked, ch 1, sk 1 dc, sc in next dc*, rep from * to * up to last 2 sts, ch 1, sk 1 dc, dc into last dc. Turn, leaving beg ch 3 of foundation row unworked. [23 shells]

Row 2: Ch 1, sc in first dc, *ch 1, shell in next sc, ch 1, sc in ch-1 sp of shell*, rep from * to * until sc has been worked into last shell, ch 1, dc in last sc.

Rep row 2 until work measures 24" from foundation row.

Spacer Band

Row 1: Ch 4, *dc in next sc, ch 1, sc in 1 ch sp of open shell, ch 1*, rep from * to *, end with ch 1, dc in last sc, turn. [47 sps, including beg ch 4]

Row 2: Ch 3, *dc in next ch-1 sp, dc in sc, dc in next sp, dc in dc*, rep from * to * up to last sp, 2 dc into sp, turn. [94 dc plus beg ch 3]

Row 3: Ch 4, sk 1 dc, dc in next dc, *ch 1, sk 1 dc, dc in next dc*, rep from * to * across, dc in top of beg ch 3 of prev row, turn. [47 ch-1 sps plus final dc]

Row 4: Ch 4, sk first dc, dc in next dc, *dc in ch-1 sp, dc in next dc*, rep from * to *, end with 2 dc in last ch-4 sp, turn. [95 dc plus beg ch 4]

Sea Fan Pattern

Row 1: Ch 5, sk 1 dc, sc in next dc, *ch 4, sk 2 dc, sc in next dc*, rep from * to *, end with sc into ch-4 sp, turn. [32 ch-4 sp, including beg ch 5]

Row 2: Ch 5, sc in first sp, *ch 4, sc in next ch-4 sp*, rep from * to *, ending with sc into 3rd ch of beg ch 5 of prev row. [32 ch-4 sps, including beg ch 5]

Row 3: Ch 5, sc in first sp, (ch 4, sc in next ch-4 sp) 4 times, *ch 2, 4 dc in next ch-4 sp, ch 2, sc in next ch-4 sp, (ch 4, sc in next ch-4 sp) 5 times*, rep from * to * 3 more times, end last rep with (ch 4, sc in next ch-4 sp) 4 times, sc in 3rd ch of beg ch 5 of prev row, turn.

Row 4: Ch 5, sc in first sp, (ch 4, sc in next ch-4 sp) 3 times, *ch 2, 2 dc in each of next 4 dc, ch 2, sc into next ch-4 sp, (ch 4, sc in next ch-4 sp) 4 times*, rep from * to * 3 more times, end last rep with sc into 3rd ch of beg ch 5 of prev row, turn.

Row 5: Ch 5, sc in first sp, (ch 4, sc in next ch-4 sp) 3 times, *2 dc into first dc, ch 1, sk 1 dc, 2 dc into next dc, ch 1, 1 dc in each of next 2 dc, ch 1, 2 dc in next dc, ch 1, sk 1 dc, 2 dc in last dc, sc in next ch-4 sp, (ch 4, sc in next ch-4 sp) 3 times*, rep from * to * 3 more times, working last sc into 3rd ch of beg ch 5 of prev row, turn.

Row 6: Ch 5, sc in first sp, (ch 4, sc in next ch-4 sp) twice, *(ch 4, sc in next ch-1 sp) 4 times, ch 4, sc in next ch-4 sp, ch 2, 4 dc in next sp, ch 2, sc in next sp*, rep from * to * twice more, then (ch 4, sc into ch-1 sp) 4 times, followed by (ch 4, sc into next ch-4 sp) 3 times, working last sc into 3rd ch of beg ch 5 of prev row, turn.

Row 7: Ch 5, sc in first sp, (4 ch, sc in next ch-4 sp) 7 times, *ch 2, 2 dc in each of next 4 dc, ch 2, sc in next ch-4 sp, (ch 4, sc in next ch-4 sp) 4 times*, rep from * to * twice more, then (ch 4, sc in next ch-4 sp) 3 times, working final sc into 3rd ch of beg ch 5 of prev row, turn.

Row 8: Ch 5, sc in first sp, (ch 4, sc in next ch-4 sp) 6 times, *2 dc into first dc, ch 1, sk 1 dc, 2 dc into next dc, ch 1, 1 dc in each of next 2 dc, ch 1, 2 dc in next dc, ch 1, sk 1 dc, 2 dc in last dc, sc in next ch-4 sp, (ch 4, sc in next sp) 3 times*, rep from * to * twice more, (ch 4, sc in next ch-4 sp) 4 times, end with sc into 3rd ch of beg ch 5 of prev row, turn.

Row 9: Ch 5, sc in first sp, (ch 4, sc into next ch-4 sp) 4 times, *ch 2, 4 dc into next ch-4 sp, ch 2, sc into next ch-4 sp, (ch 4, sc into next ch-1 sp) 4 times, ch 4, sc in next ch-4 sp*, rep from * to * twice more, then ch 2, 4 dc into next ch-4 sp, ch 2, sc into next ch-4 sp, (4 ch, sc in next ch-4 sp) 3 times, ch 4, end with sc in 3rd ch of beg ch 5, turn.

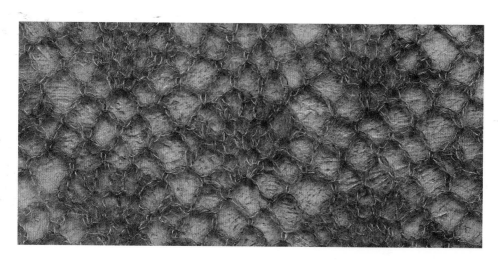

Rep rows 4–9 twice, then rep rows 4–8 once more.

Next row: Ch 5, sc into first sp, (ch 4, sc) into rem sp, end with (ch 4, sc) in 3rd ch of beg ch 5 of prev row. Fasten off.

Stole (Second Half)

Work as first half, but do not fasten off.

Invisible Join

Place both halves on a flat surface with the sea-fan sections facing each other, the half just finished on the left, with the yarn still attached and nearest you. The other half should be on the right, with the edge ½ space facing the edge whole space of the left half (see diagram at right). Ch 2, pull a lp through the ½ sp and finish as sc. Cont across with *ch 2, make sc through lp on opposite side*, rep from * to *, alternating sides. At end, make sc in 3rd ch of beg ch 5 of ½ sp (on left), then ch 2, make sc at opposite edge, and fasten off.

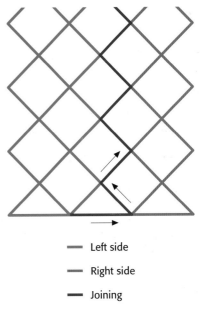

— Left side

— Right side

— Joining

Arrows show direction of working.

Finishing

Weave in all ends, dampen stole, and pin out to finished measurements.

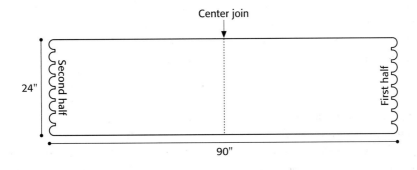

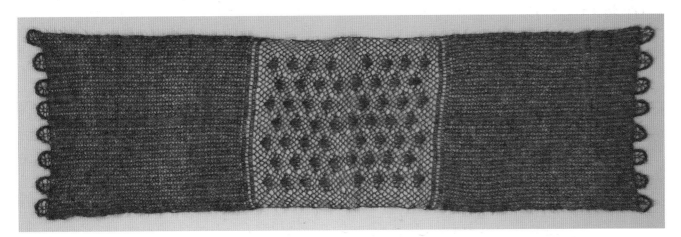

Elegant Evening Shawl

By Janet Rehfeldt

Be the toast of the town in this elegant evening shawl. The glittery jewel tones and bits of metallic yarn will glimmer and shine, elegantly wrapping you in luxury. Worked in 10 different yarns, this shawl is self-fringing so there are no ends to work in.

Skill Level: Intermediate ◼◼◼▢

Approximate Dimensions

8" wide x 56" long (excluding fringe)

Featured Stitches

Back loop (bl)
Chain (ch)
Front loop (fl)
Slip stitch (sl st)

Pattern Stitch

Row 1 (RS): Turn work, reattach yarn at edge of work, sl st in fl of first st, sl st in fl of each st across, fasten off.

Row 2 (WS): Turn work, reattach yarn at edge of work, sl st in bl of first st, sl st in bl of each st across, fasten off.

Materials

A: 1 ball of Metallic FX from Berroco (85% rayon, 15% metallic; 85 yds; 25 g), color 1012 ③

B: 1 ball of Metallic FX from Berroco, color 1001 ③

C: 1 ball of Metallic FX from Berroco, color 1003 ③

D: 1 ball of Chinchilla from Berroco (100% rayon; 77 yds; 50 g), color 5363 ⑤

E: 1 ball of Optik from Berroco (48% cotton, 21% acrylic, 20% mohair, 8% metallic, 3% polyester; 87 yds; 50 g), color 4950 ⑤

F: 3 balls of Plume FX from Berroco (100% polyester; 63 yds; 20 g), color 6716 ③

G: 1 ball of Mosaic FX from Berroco (100% nylon; 78 yds; 25 g), color 4615 ④

H: 1 ball of Mirror FX from Berroco (100% polyester; 60 yds; 10 g), color 9003 ①

I: 1 ball of Mirror FX from Berroco, color 9001 ①

J: 1 ball of Glacé from Berroco (100% rayon; 75 yds; 50 g), color 2564 ④

Size M-13 (9 mm) crochet hook (or size required to obtain gauge)

Fray Check (optional)

Gauge

10 sts = 4" using size M-13 (9 mm) crochet hook over patt st

> **NOTE:** When changing from one yarn to the next, leave 8" tails. These tails form the fringes at each end.

Shawl

Row 1: With A and F held tog, ch 145 sts, working in bottom hump of ch, sl st in 2nd ch from hook, sl st in each ch across, fasten off.

Row 2: Turn work, reattach yarn at edge of work, sl st in bl of first st, sl st in bl of each st across, fasten off.

Changing yarns as listed below, work rows 1 and 2 of patt st in each listed yarn. Where more than one yarn is listed, work the 2 strands tog as one. Cont to fasten off at end of each row, leaving 8" tails, turning work, and attaching yarn at beg of each new row.

A/F; D; E; F/G; B; C/H; F/J; D/H; A; B; F/G; E; C/H; F/J; D; C; B/I; E; F/G; F/J; C; D; A/F.

Fasten off. Lightly steam. If necessary, trim fringe even.

> **NOTE:** You may need to place a small dab of Fray Check on the tips of the Metallic FX fringe to prevent fraying.

Wrapped in Bronze

By Janet Rehfeldt

Whether you choose cool bronze or vibrant reds, this scarf is fabulous. With its elegant stitch structure of crocheted garter-stitch panels in a soft slub and accents of short, fizzy strands of eyelash, you'll be the talk of the town when you wear it. The scarf looks equally good in the office or paired with jeans. Make it in your choice of two widths.

Skill Level: Easy ◼◼☐☐

Approximate Dimensions

Wide scarf: 4½" wide x 39" long

Narrow scarf: 3" wide x 46½" long

Featured Stitches

Back loop (bl)
Chain (ch)
Front loop (fl)
Single crochet (sc)
Slip stitch (sl st)

Materials

A: 1 ball of Fizz from Crystal Palace Yarns (100% poly-ester; 120 yds; 50 g), color 9152 or 7128 (4)

B: 1 ball of Waikiki from Crystal Palace Yarns (70% rayon, 30% cotton; 105 yds; 50 g), color 2890 or 2645 (4)

Size H-8 (5 mm) crochet hook (or size required to obtain gauge)

Gauge

14 sc = 4" using size H-8 (5 mm) crochet hook

> **NOTE:** *Scarf is worked from side to side. Directions are written for wide scarf with narrow version in parentheses. (Narrow version is longer, so there are more stitches for the narrow scarf.) Work all slip stitches loosely but not sloppily.*

Scarf

Row 1: With A, ch 138 (164), working in bottom hump of ch, sc in 2nd ch from hook, sc in each ch across, turn. [137 (163) sc]

Rows 2–6: Ch 1, sc in first sc, sc in each sc across, turn.

Row 7: Change to B, ch 1, loosely sl st in fl of first sc, sl st in fl of each sc across, turn. [137 (163) sl sts]

Row 8: Ch 1, loosely sl st in bl of first sl st, sl st in bl of each sl st across, turn.

Row 9: Ch 1, loosely sl st in fl of first sl st, sl st in fl of each sl st across, turn.

Rows 10–14: Rep rows 8 and 9 twice, then rep row 8 once more.

Row 15: Ch 1, sc in fl of first sl st, sc in fl of each sl st across, changing to A at end of row.

Wide scarf: Rep rows 2–15 once, then rows 2–6 once more.

Narrow scarf: Rep rows 2–6 once.

Fasten off and weave in ends.

Fabulously Flirty Poncho

By Janet Rehfeldt

Two basic rectangles are all it takes for this short, cropped, updated, and flirty poncho. Using a yarn with little tufts of flat ribbon makes this easy poncho appear to have small flower petals, creating the texture. It's the perfect companion to a tank top and jeans or a skirt.

Skill Level: Easy ◼◼◻◻

Approximate Dimensions

20" wide x 24½" long

Featured Stitches

Chain (ch)
Extended single crochet (esc), page 16

Materials

4 balls of Dune from Sirdar (100% nylon; 109 yds/100 m; 50 g), color 110 ⑤

Size M-13 (9 mm) crochet hook (or size required to obtain gauge)

Size I-9 (5.5 mm) crochet hook for fringe

Gauge

10 sts x 4 rows = 4" using M-13 (9 mm) crochet hook, unstretched

> **NOTE:** *Plastic hooks work best with this yarn. Attach new yarn at side edges only, not in center of a row. Measure both gauge swatch and garment on a smooth, flat surface because yarn stretches.*

Panels (Make 2)

Row 1: With size M-13 hook, ch 24, esc in 2nd ch from hook, esc in each ch, turn. [23 esc]

Row 2 (RS): Ch 1, esc in first esc, esc in each esc across, turn.

Rep row 2 until piece measures 24½".

Fringe

Cut yarn into 132 lengths of 12" each for 22 fringes. Holding 6 strands tog, fold fringe in half to form a lp; beg at lower corner, insert size I-9 crochet hook through back of work to front, place lp onto hook, draw lp through piece, then bring ends through lp and tighten. Evenly space 11 fringe tassels along bottom edge of each front and back piece.

Finishing

Sew shoulder seams tog, keeping center 11¼" open for neck opening.

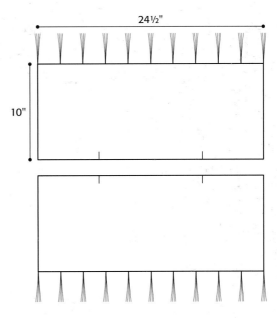

Fair Isle Set

By Kathleen Stuart

This beautiful Fair Isle patterned set, worked in wonderfully soft alpaca yarn, will delight most anyone on your gift list. The elegant square-and-dot motif is worked while carrying the yarn along so there are fewer ends to weave in.

Skill Level: Intermediate ◼◼◼◻

Approximate Dimensions

Hat: To fit 19"–24" head circumference

Mittens: Small/Medium (Medium/Large) to fit 5–7 (8–9)" hand circumference

Scarf: 8¼" wide x 56" long

Materials

A: Baby Alpaca DK from Plymouth Yarn (100% baby alpaca; 125 yds; 50 g), color 100 🧶

B: Baby Alpaca DK from Plymouth Yarn, color 500 🧶

C: Baby Alpaca DK from Plymouth Yarn, color 401 🧶

Hat: 1 ball each of A, B, and C

Mittens: 1 ball each of A, B, and C

Scarf: 2 balls each of A, B, and C

K-10.5 (6.5 mm) crochet hook (or size required to obtain gauge)

Featured Stitches

Chain (ch)
Double crochet (dc)
Single crochet (sc)
Slip stitch (sl st)

Gauge

15½ sts x 16 rows = 4" in color patt using size K-10.5 (6.5 mm) crochet hook

Hat

> **NOTE:** *Hat is worked in the round from brim to crown. Each round is joined and then turned as if worked in rows. Carry yarn on wrong side of work, allowing the unused yarn to strand along the back. Do not work the unused colors into the work.*

With B, ch 67 loosely, sl st in first ch to form a ring.

Rnd 1 (WS): Ch 1, sc in same ch as sl st and in each ch around, sl st to first sc to join, changing to C, turn. [67 sc]

Rnd 2 (RS): Ch 1, sc in each st around, sl st to first sc to join, changing to A in sl st, turn.

Rnd 3: Ch 1, sc in first sc, (ch 1, sk next sc, sc in next sc) around, sl st to first sc to join, changing to C in sl st, turn.

Rnd 4: Ch 1, sc in first sc, working in front of ch 1, (dc in sc 1 rnd below next ch 1, sc in next sc) around, sl st to first sc to join, changing to B in last sl st, turn.

Rnd 5: Ch 1, sc in each st around, sl st to first sc to join, changing to A in sl st, turn.

Rnd 6: Ch 1, sc in each st around, sl st to first sc to join, changing to C in sl st, turn.

Rnd 7: Ch 1, sc in first 2 sc, ch 1, sk next sc, sc in next sc, ch 1, *sk next sc, sc in next 3 sts, ch 1, sk next sc, sc in next sc, ch 1*, rep from * to * around to last 3 sts, sk next sc, sc in last 2 sts, sl st to first sc to join, changing to A in sl st, turn.

Rnd 8: Ch 1, sc in first 2 sc, working in front of next ch 1, dc in sc 1 rnd below ch 1, sc in next sc, working in front of next ch 1, dc in sc 1 rnd below ch 1, *sc in next 3 sc, working in front of next ch 1, dc in sc 1 rnd below ch 1, sc in next sc, working in front of next ch 1, dc in sc 1 rnd below ch 1*, rep from * to * around to last 2 sc, sc in last 2 sc, sl st to first sc to join, changing to B in sl st, turn.

Rnd 9: Ch 1, sc in first sc, *ch 1, sk next sc, sc in next 3 sc, ch 1, sk next sc, sc in next sc*, rep from * to * around, sl st to first sc to join, changing to A in sl st, turn.

Rnd 10: Ch 1, sc in first sc, *working in front of next ch 1, dc in sc 1 rnd below ch 1, ch 1, sk next sc, sc in esc, ch 1, sk next sc, working in front of next ch 1, dc in sc 1 rnd below ch 1, sc in next sc*, rep from * to * around, sl st to first sc to join, changing to B in sl st, turn.

Rnd 11: Ch 1, sc in first sc, *ch 1, sk next dc, working in back of next ch 1, dc in sc 1 rnd below ch 1, sc in next sc, working in back of next ch 1, dc in sc 1 rnd below ch 1, ch 1, sk next dc, sc in next sc*, rep from * to * around, sl st to first sc to join, changing to A in sl st, turn.

Rnd 12: Ch 1, sc in first sc, *working in front of next ch 1, dc in dc 1 rnd below ch 1, sc in next 3 sts, working in front of next ch 1, dc in dc 1 rnd below ch 1, sc in next sc*, rep from * to * around, sl st to first sc to join, changing to C in sl st, turn.

Rnds 13 and 14: Rep rnds 7 and 8.

Rnd 15: Ch 1, sc in each sc around, sl st to first sc to join, changing to C in sl st, turn.

Rnds 16–19: Rep rnds 2–5.

Rnd 20: Ch 1, sc in each st around, sl st to first sc to join, changing to B in sl st, turn.

Rnd 21: Ch 1, sc in first 2 sts, ch 3 (loosely), *sk next 3 sts, sc in next st, ch 3*, rep from * to * around to last 5 sts, sk next 3 sts, sc in last 2 sts, changing to A in last sc, turn.

Rnd 22: Ch 1, sc in first 2 sts, working in front of ch 3, (dc in next st 1 rnd below ch 3) 3 times, *sc in next st, working in front of ch 3, (dc in next st 1 rnd below ch 3) 3 times*, rep from * to * around to last 2 sc, sc in last 2 sc, changing to C in last sc, turn.

Rnd 23: Ch 1, sc in first st, ch 2, sk next 2 sts, sc in next st, *ch 3, sk next 3 sts, sc in next st*, rep from * to * around to last 3 sts, ch 2, sk next 2 sts, sc in last st, changing to A in last sc, turn.

Rnd 24: Ch 1, sc in first st, working in front of ch 2, (dc in next st 1 rnd below ch 2) twice, sc in next st, *working in front of ch 3, (dc in next st 1 rnd below ch 3) 3 times, sc in next st*, rep from * to * around to last ch 2, working in front of ch 2, (dc in next st 1 rnd below ch 2) twice, sc in last st, changing to B in last sc, turn.

Rnds 25–36: Rep rnds 21–24 three more times (you'll have 4 black and 4 gray spotted rnds). Do not turn at end of rnd 36.

Rnd 37: Ch 1, sc2tog around, sc in last st, join with sl st in first sc to join.

Finish off and draw yarn through sts, close up opening with a yarn needle. Weave in ends.

Mittens (Make 2)

> **NOTE:** *Mittens are worked in the round. Each round is joined and then turned as if worked in rows. Carry yarn on wrong side of work.*

With B, ch 25 (31) loosely, sl st in first ch to form a ring.

Rnd 1 (WS): Ch 1, sc in same ch as sl st, sc in each ch around, sl st to first sc to join, changing to C, turn. [25 (31) sc]

Rnd 2 (RS): Ch 1, sc in each st around, sl st to first sc to join, changing to A in sl st, turn.

Rnd 3: Ch 1, sc in first sc, (ch 1, sk next sc, sc in next sc) around, sl st to first sc to join, changing to C in sl st, turn.

Rnd 4: Ch 1, sc in first sc, working in front of ch 1, (dc in sc 1 rnd below next ch 1, sc in next sc) around, sl st to first sc to join, changing to B in sl st, turn.

Rnd 5: Ch 1, sc in each st around, sl st to first sc to join, changing to A in sl st, turn.

Rnd 6: Ch 1, sc in each st around, sl st to first sc to join, changing to C in sl st, turn.

Rnd 7: Ch 1, sc in first 2 sc, ch 1, sk next sc, sc in next sc, ch 1, *sk next sc, sc in next 3 sts, ch 1, sk next sc, sc in next sc, ch 1*, rep from * to * around to last 3 sts, sk next sc, sc in last 2 sts, sl st to first sc to join, changing to A in sl st, turn.

Rnd 8: Ch 1, sc in first 2 sc, working in front of next ch 1, dc in sc 1 rnd below ch 1, sc in next sc, working in front of next ch 1, dc in sc 1 rnd below ch 1, *sc in next 3 sc, working in front of next ch 1, dc in sc 1 rnd below ch 1, sc in next sc, working in front of next ch 1, dc in sc 1 rnd below ch 1*, rep from * to * around to last 2 sc, sc in last 2 sc, sl st to first sc to join, changing to B in sl st, turn.

Rnd 9: Ch 1, sc in first sc, *ch 1, sk next sc, sc in next 3 sc, ch 1, sk next sc, sc in next sc*, rep from * to * around, sl st to first sc to join, changing to A in sl st, turn.

Rnd 10: Ch 1, sc in first sc, *working in front of next ch 1, dc in sc 1 rnd below ch 1, ch 1, sk next sc, sc in esc, ch 1, sk next sc, working in front of next ch 1, dc in sc 1 rnd below ch 1, sc in next sc*, rep from * to * around, sl st to first sc to join, changing to B in sl st, turn.

Rnd 11: Ch 1, sc in first sc, *ch 1, sk next dc, working in back of next ch 1, dc in sc 1 rnd below ch 1, sc in next sc, working in back of next ch 1, dc in sc 1 rnd below ch 1, ch 1, sk next dc, sc in next sc*, rep from * to * around, sl st to first sc to join, changing to A in sl st, turn.

Rnd 12: Ch 1, sc in first sc, *working in front of next ch 1, dc in dc 1 rnd below ch 1, sc in next 3 sts, working in front of next ch 1, dc in dc 1 rnd below ch 1, sc in next sc*, rep from * to * around, sl st to first sc to join, changing to C in sl st, turn.

Rnds 13 and 14: Rep rnds 7 and 8.

Rnd 15: Ch 1, sc in each sc around, sl st to first sc to join, changing to C in sl st, turn.

Rnds 16–18: Rep rnds 2–4.

Rnd 19: Ch 1, [sc in first 5 (6) sts, 2 sc in next st] 4 times, sc in last 1 (3) sts, sl st to first sc to join, changing to A in sl st, turn. [29 (35) sts]

Rnd 20: Ch 1, sc in each sc around, sl st to first sc to join, turn.

Right Mitten

Rnd 21: Ch 1, sc in first 10 (12) sts, ch 6, sk next 8 (10) sts (thumb hole), sc in last 11 (13) sts, sl st to first sc to join, turn. [21 (25) sc; 6 (6) ch]

Left Mitten

Rnd 21: Ch 1, sc in first 11 (13) sts, ch 6, sk next 8 (10) sts (thumb hole), sc in last 10 (13) sts, sl st to first sc to join, turn. [21 (25) sc; 6 (6) ch]

Both Mittens

Rnd 22: Ch 1, sc in each st around, sl st to first sc to join, changing to B in sl st, turn. [27 (31) sts]

Rnd 23: Ch 1, sc in first 2 sts, ch 3 (loosely), *sk next 3 sts, sc in next st, ch 3*, rep from * to * around to last 5 sts, sk next 3 sts, sc in last 2 sts, changing to A in last sc, turn.

Rnd 24: Ch 1, sc in first 2 sts, working in front of ch 3, (dc in next st 1 rnd below ch 3) 3 times, *sc in next st, working in front of ch 3, (dc in next st 1 rnd below ch 3) 3 times*, rep from * to * around to last 2 sc, sc in last 2 sc, changing to C in last sc, turn.

Rnd 25: Ch 1, sc in first st, ch 2, sk next 2 sts, sc in next st, *ch 3, sk next 3 sts, sc in next st*, rep from * to * around to last 3 sts, ch 2, sk next 2 sts, sc in last st, changing to A, turn.

Rnd 26: Ch 1, sc in first st, working in front of ch 2, (dc in next st 1 rnd below ch 2) twice, sc in next st, *working in front of ch 3, (dc in next st 1 rnd below ch 3) 3 times, sc in next st*, rep from * to * around to last ch 2, working in front of ch 2, (dc in next st 1 rnd below ch 2) twice, sc in last st, changing to B in last sc, turn.

Small/Medium Size Only

Rnds 27–40: Rep rnds 23–26 three times, then rep rounds 23 and 24 once more. [5 black and 4 gray spotted rnds]

Rnd 41: Ch 1, do not turn, sc2tog around, sc in last st, join with sl st in first sc to join. Fasten off and draw yarn through sts to close up opening.

Medium/Large Size Only

Rnds 27–42: Rep rnds 23–26 four times. [5 black and 5 gray spotted rnds]

Rnd 43: Ch 1, do not turn, sc2tog around, sc in last st, join with sl st in first sc to join. Fasten off and draw yarn through sts to close up opening.

Thumb

> **NOTE:** *Do not turn; do not join rounds.*

Rnd 1: With A, sc in first skipped st of rnd 20, sc in next 7 (9) skipped sts, sc into base of each of the 6 ch. [14 (16) sc]

Rnds 2–13 (14): Sc in each st around.

Rnd 14 (15): Sc2tog around. [7 (8) sc]

Fasten off and draw yarn through sts; weave tail through sts to close up opening. Weave in ends.

Scarf

> **NOTE:** *There are many color changes. The instructions will state when to strand yarn to the wrong side when necessary; otherwise, carry yarn along the edges. To strand yarn, carry the unused yarn color along the wrong side of the work, working over it when doing single crochet. Do not pull yarn too tightly, as it will cause the work to pucker.*

Row 1 (WS): With B, ch 32 loosely, sc in 2nd ch from hook and in each ch across, changing to C in last sc, strand B on wrong side while working next row, turn. [31 sc]

Row 2 (RS): Ch 1, sc in each st across, changing to A in last sc, strand C on wrong side while working next row, turn.

Row 3: Ch 1, sc in first sc, (ch 1, sk next sc, sc in next sc) across, changing to C in last sc, turn.

Row 4: Ch 1, sc in first sc, working in front of ch 1, (dc in sc 1 row below next ch 1, sc in next sc) across, changing to B in last sc, turn.

Row 5: Ch 1, sc in each st across, changing to A in last sc, strand B on wrong side while working next row, turn.

Row 6: Ch 1, sc in each st across, changing to C in last sc, strand A on wrong side while working next row, turn.

Row 7: Ch 1, sc in first 2 sc, ch 1, sk next sc, sc in next sc, ch 1, *sk next sc, sc in next 3 sts, ch 1, sk next sc, sc in next sc, ch 1*, rep from * to * across to last 3 sts, sk next sc, sc in last 2 sts, changing to A in last sc, strand C on wrong side while working next row, turn.

Row 8: Ch 1, sc in first 2 sc, working in front of next ch 1, dc in sc 1 row below ch 1, sc in next sc, working in front of next ch 1, dc in sc 1 row below ch 1, *sc in next 3 sc, working in front of next ch 1, dc in sc 1 row below ch 1, sc in next sc, working in front

of next ch 1, dc in sc 1 row below ch 1*, rep from * to * across to last 2 sc, sc in last 2 sc, changing to B in last sc, strand A on wrong side while working next row, turn.

Row 9: Ch 1, sc in first sc, *ch 1, sk next sc, sc in next 3 sc, ch 1, sk next sc, sc in next sc*, rep from * to * across, changing to A in last sc, strand B on wrong side while working next row, turn.

Row 10: Ch 1, sc in first sc, *working in front of next ch 1, dc in sc 1 row below ch 1, ch 1, sk next sc, sc in next sc, ch 1, sk next sc, working in front of next ch 1, dc in sc 1 row below ch 1, sc in next sc*, rep from * to * across, changing to B in last sc, strand A on wrong side while working next row, turn.

Row 11: Ch 1, sc in first sc, *ch 1, sk next dc, working in back of next ch 1, dc in sc 1 row below ch 1, sc in next sc, working in back of next ch 1, dc in sc 1 row below ch 1, ch 1, sk next dc, sc in next sc*, rep from * to * across, changing to A in last sc, strand B on wrong side while working next row, turn.

Row 12: Ch 1, sc in first sc, *working in front of next ch 1, dc in dc 1 row below ch 1, sc in next 3 sts, working in front of next ch 1, dc in dc 1 row below ch 1, sc in next sc*, rep from * to * across, changing to C in last sc, strand A on wrong side while working next row, turn.

Rows 13 and 14: Rep rows 7 and 8.

Row 15: Ch 1, sc in each sc across, changing to C in last sc, strand B on wrong side while working next row, turn.

Rows 16–19: Rep rows 2–5.

Row 20: Ch 1, sc in each sc across, changing to B in last sc, strand A on wrong side while working next row, turn.

Row 21: Ch 1, sc in first 2 sts, ch 3 (loosely), *sk next 3 sts, sc in next st, ch 3*, rep from * to * across to last 5 sts, sk next 3 sts, sc in last 2 sts, changing to A in last sc, strand B on wrong side while working next row, turn.

Row 22: Ch 1, sc in first 2 sts, working in front of ch 3, (dc in next st 1 row below ch 3) 3 times, *sc in next st, working in front of ch 3, (dc in next st 1 row below ch 3) 3 times*, rep from * to * across to last 2 sc, sc in last 2 sc, changing to C in last sc, strand A on wrong side while working next row, turn.

Row 23: Ch 1, sc in first st, ch 2, sk next 2 sts, sc in next st, *ch 3, sk next 3 sts, sc in next st*, rep from * to * across to last 3 sts, ch 2, sk next 2 sts, sc in last st, changing to A, strand C on wrong side while working next row, turn.

Row 24: Ch 1, sc in first st, working in front of ch 2, (dc in next st 1 row below ch 2) twice, sc in next st, *working in front of ch 3, (dc in next st 1 row below ch 3) 3 times, sc in next st*, rep from * to * across to last ch 2, working in front of ch 2, (dc in next st 1 row below ch 2) twice, sc in last st, changing to B in last sc, strand A on wrong side while working next row, turn.

Rows 25–46: Rep rows 21–24 five times, then rep rows 21 and 22 once more. [7 black and 6 gray spotted rows]

Row 47: Ch 1, sc in each sc across, changing to B in last sc, turn.

Rows 48–92: Rep rows 2–46, using C for B and B for C throughout.

Row 93: Ch 1, sc in each sc across, changing to C in last sc, turn.

Rows 94–138: Rep rows 2–46, keeping same colors as in instructions.

Row 139: Ch 1, sc in each sc across, changing to B in last sc, turn.

Rows 140–184: Rep rows 2–46, using C for B and B for C throughout.

Row 185: Ch 1, sc in each sc across, changing to C in last sc, turn.

Rows 186–203: Rep rows 2–19, using same colors.

Fasten off at end of row 203. Weave in ends.

Blue Suede Set

By Janet Rehfeldt

This plush hat and scarf set is bound to become one of your favorites. Made with the cluster stitch and a yarn that has the look and feel of suede, it's wonderfully soft and, best of all, the scarf is self-fringing. The stitch structure and yarn make the hat stretchy enough to fit most teen and adult women.

Skill Level: Easy ◖◼◻◻

Approximate Dimensions

Scarf: 4½" wide x 48" long (excluding fringe)

Hat: To fit 18"–23" head circumference

Featured Stitches

Chain (ch)
Double crochet (dc)
Reverse single crochet (rsc)
Single crochet (sc)
Slip stitch (sl st)

Special Stitches

Cluster stitch: Work (1 sc, 1 dc) into same st.

Cluster decrease: Insert hook into next sc, yo, pull through st, insert hook into next dc, yo, pull through st, yo, pull through 3 lps on hook, yo, insert hook into same dc, yo, pull through st, insert hook into next sc, yo, pull through st, yo, pull through 2 lps on hook, yo, pull through 3 lps on hook—cluster dec made.

Materials

Hat

1 ball of Lion Suede from Lion Brand (100% polyester; 122 yds/110 m; 3 oz/85 g), color 110 ⑤

Size K-10.5 (6.5 mm) crochet hook (or size required to obtain gauge)

1 stitch marker

Scarf

1 ball of Lion Suede from Lion Brand (100% polyester; 122 yds/110 m; 3 oz/85 g) color 110 **⑤**

Size N-15 (10 mm) crochet hook (or size required to obtain gauge)

Gauge

Hat: 5 clusters = 4" using size K-10.5 (6.5 mm) crochet hook

Scarf: 3½ clusters = 4" using size N-15 (10 mm) crochet hook

Hat

> *NOTE: Hat is worked in the round from brim to crown. Brim is worked from the wrong side, so when it is turned up, the right side of the work shows. Do not chain 1 at the beginning of rounds or slip stitch rounds closed unless otherwise instructed.*

Brim

Foundation row (WS): With size K-10.5 hook, ch 47, working in bottom hump of ch, sc in 2nd ch from hook, sc in each ch across, do not turn. [46 sc]

Rnd 1: Sl st in first sc of row 1 to form a ring, pm to mark beg of rnd, sc in next sc, *sl st in next sc, sc in next sc*, rep from * to * around.

Rnd 2: Sc in first sl st of previous rnd, sl st in next sc, *sc in next sl st, sl st in next sc*, rep from * to * around.

Rnd 3: Sl st in first sc of previous rnd, sc in next sl st, *sl st in next sc, sc in next sl st*, rep from * to * around.

Rnds 4 and 5: Rep rnds 2 and 3, sl st in first st to close rnd at end of rnd 5. Remove marker and turn work inside out.

Rnd 6 (RS): Ch 1, (sc, dc) in first st, sk next st, *(sc, dc) in next st, sk next st*, rep from * to * around. Replace marker to mark beg of rnds. Do not turn work on this or following rnds. [23 clusters]

Rnd 7: (Sc, dc) in first sc, sk next dc, *(sc, dc) in next sc, sk next dc*, rep from * to * around.

Rep rnd 7 until hat measures 6" from beg.

Crown

Rnd 1: [(Sc, dc) in next sc, sk next dc] twice, *cluster dec, [(sc, dc) in next sc, sk next dc] 3 times*, rep from * to * twice, cluster dec, [(sc, dc) in next sc, sk next dc] twice, cluster dec. [18 clusters]

Rnd 2: *(Sc, dc) in next sc, sk next dc*, rep from * to * around.

Rnd 3: [(Sc, dc) in next sc, sk next dc] 3 times, *cluster dec, [(sc, dc) in next sc, sk next dc] 3 times*, rep from * to * around. [15 clusters]

Rnd 4: Rep rnd 2 of crown.

Rnd 5: *(Sc, dc) in next sc, sk next dc, cluster dec*, rep from * to * around. [10 clusters]

Rnd 6: Rep rnd 2 of crown.

Rnd 7: *Cluster dec*, rep from * to * around, sl st in first st to close rnd. [5 clusters]

Fasten off, leaving an 8" tail.

Thread tail in and out of top of sts in rnd 7, pull tight to close top of hat. Secure with a sewing st. Attach yarn to bottom of foundation row. Work 1 rnd of rev sc. Fasten off, weave in ends. Fold brim up at rnd 5.

Scarf

> *NOTE: Scarf is worked from side to side with the right side always facing you.*

Row 1 (RS): With size N-15 hook and leaving a 12" tail, loosely ch 84. Working in bottom hump of ch, (sc, dc) in 2nd ch from hook, sk next ch, *(sc, dc) in next ch, sk next ch*, rep from * to * across to last ch, sc in last ch, fasten off, leaving a 12" tail. Do not turn. [41 clusters, 1 sc]

Row 2: Attach yarn at beg of prev row with a knot, leaving a 12" tail. (Sc, dc) in first sc, sk next dc, *(sc, dc) in next sc, sk next dc*, rep from * to * across to last sc, sc in last sc, fasten off, leaving a 12" tail. Do not turn.

Rep row 2 six times. Trim fringe if desired.

Shell Collar and Flower Pin

By Karen Klemp

Accessorize your blouses, sweaters, and tops with this beautiful collar and coordinating flower pin made with a wonderful slubbed rayon yarn. You can fasten the collar in several ways. Use the coordinating flower pin, sew a large decorative button on one side of the neck edge, or use a beautiful hair stick, stickpin, or brooch from your collection.

Skill Level: Easy ◖◼◻◻

Approximate Dimensions

18" around first row at neck

Featured Stitches

Chain (ch)
Double crochet (dc)
Front loop (fl)
Single crochet (sc)
Slip stitch (sl st)

Special Stitches

V-stitch: (dc, ch 1, dc) into same stitch

Shell: (2 dc, ch 1, 2 dc) into same stitch

Large Shell: (3 dc, ch 1, 3 dc) into same stitch

Materials

Collar

A: 1 ball of Cleo from Muench Yarns (87% viscose, 13% metal; 62 yds; 1.75 oz/50 g), color 381151

B: 1 ball of Metal from Trendsetter Yarns (100% polyester; 72 yds/77 m; 20 g), color 20

Size K-10.5 (6.5 mm) crochet hook (or size required to obtain gauge)

Size L-11 (8 mm) crochet hook

Button, hair stick, stickpin, or brooch (optional)

Flower

1 ball of Cleo from Muench Yarns (87% viscose, 13% metal; 62 yds; 1.75 oz/50 g) color 381151

Size K-10.5 (6.5 mm) crochet hook

Pin back or stickpin (optional)

> *NOTE: If your eyelash yarn comes wrapped on a foam core, you can use it by just unwinding from the outside. If it has no core, find the outside of the ball, unwind a few feet, and wrap that amount securely around the outside. Then fish inside the ball for the other end of the yarn, and pull it out from the inside. It may come out in a big clump that you then need to untangle and use first, but if you just start using the entire ball from the outside, you may find about halfway through that the inside and outside strands are twisting around each other, causing a major problem.*

Gauge

12 sc = 4" using size K-10.5 (6.5 mm) crochet hook

Gauge isn't too important for this pattern. The collar should drape nicely and be soft to the touch. If your stitches are very tight, creating a stiff fabric, change to a larger hook.

> *NOTE: If you've never worked with slubbed or thin eyelash yarns before, see "Novelty Yarns" on page 6.*

Collar

With A and size K-10.5 hook, ch 40 (or an even number of stitches that will fit comfortably around your neck). The first row of our model measures 18".

Row 1: Sc in 2nd ch from hook and in each ch across, turn. [39 sc]

Row 2: Ch 4, dc in first st (to form first V-stitch), *sk 1 st, work V-stitch in next ch*, rep from * to * across, turn. [20 V-stitches]

Row 3: Sl st in ch-1 sp of first V-stitch, ch 3, 1 dc, ch 1, 2 dc in same sp, work shell in center of each V-stitch across, turn.

Row 4: Sl st in first 2 dc and in ch-1 sp, ch 3, 2 dc, ch 1, 3 dc in same sp, work large shell in center of each shell across, turn.

Row 5: Change to size L-11 hook. Holding 1 strand each of A and B tog, ch 1, sc in first st, *ch 1, sk 1 st, sc in next st*, rep from * to * across.

Fasten off and weave in ends. You can fasten your collar in several ways. Sew a large decorative button on one side of the neck edge; use a beautiful hair stick, stickpin, or brooch from your collection to pin it; or add the coordinating flower, using the pattern below.

Ruffled Flower

Rnd 1: With size K-10.5 hook, ch 2, 12 sc in 2nd ch from hook, join with sl st in fl of first sc.

Rnd 2: Working in fl only, *ch 3, sl st in next st*, rep from * to * around.

Rnd 3: Working in unused back lps of rnd 1, work 2 sc in each st around, join with sl st in fl of first sc.

Rnd 4: Working in fl only of rnd 3, *ch 5, sl st in next st*, rep from * to * around.

Rnd 5: Working in unused back lps of rnd 3, *1 sc in next st, 2 sc in next st*, rep from * to * around, join with sl st in fl of first sc.

Rnd 6: Working in fl only of rnd 5, *ch 7, sl st in next st*, rep from * to * around. Sl st to unused back lp of first st.

Rnd 7: Working in unused back lps of rnd 5, *ch 9, sl st in next st*, rep from * to * around. Fasten off and weave in ends. Sew a pin back to back of flower or fasten flower to collar with a stickpin.

All That Glitters

By Janet Rehfeldt

All that glitters isn't really gold—it's sequin! Be the belle of the ball and add twinkle and glitz to your evening out with little bits of sequin that catch the light. The carry-along yarn has sequins attached to the thread, so you don't have to strand them yourself—just one more little marvel of the novelty yarns available.

Skill Level: Intermediate ◀■■▢

Approximate Dimensions

5½" wide x 36" long

Featured Stitches

Chain (ch)
Extended single crochet (esc), page 16
Slip stitch (sl st)

Materials

A: 1 ball of Eros from Plymouth Yarn (100% nylon; 165 yds/180 m; 1.75 oz/50 g), color 2024 (4)

OR

1 ball of Eros Glitz from Plymouth (86% nylon, 10% rayon, 4% lurex; 158 yds/172 m; 1.75 oz/50 g), color 66 (4)

B: 1 ball of Mirror FX from Berroco (100% polyester; 60 yds/65 m; 10 g), color 9003 or 9002 (1)

Size J-10 (6 mm) crochet hook (or size required to obtain gauge)

Gauge

11 esc = 4" using size J-10 (6 mm) crochet hook

> *NOTE: Work all slip stitches very loosely. Carry B along the edge by working the beginning chain 1 with A and B held together to keep the thread from hanging loose along the side edge to catch and break. B will not always be at the same side edge of the scarf.*

Scarf

Row 1: With A, ch 15, esc in 2nd ch from hook, esc in each ch across, turn. [14 esc]

Row 2: Ch 1, esc in first esc, esc in each esc across, turn.

Row 3: Add B, with A and B held tog ch 1, loosely sl st in first esc, loosely sl st in each esc across, turn. Drop B.

Rows 4 and 5: Ch 1, esc in first esc, esc in each esc across, turn.

Rep rows 3–5 until you run out of yarn, ending with row 5. Fasten off, weave in ends.

Reversible Ripple Scarf

By Darla J. Fanton

Whether your taste runs to limes and loops or roses and lace, this scarf serves up maximum fashion appeal. Fabric made with the double-ended crochet hook is reversible, giving you even more options each time you wear your scarf.

Skill Level: Easy ◀■□□

Approximate Dimensions

4" wide x 47" long

Featured Stitches

Chain (ch)
Cluster (cl)
Single crochet (sc)
Slip stitch (sl st)

Special Stitch

Single crochet loop (sc loop): Pick up lp in designated place, yo, and draw through 1 lp on hook.

Materials

Loopy Lime Scarf

A: 1 ball of Sevilla from Katia (100% nylon; 153 yds/140 m; 1¾ oz/50 g), color 56 ◀4▶

B: 2 balls of Fabu from Muench Yarns (90% viscose, 10% polyester; 79 yds/72 m; 1¾ oz/50 g), color 4315 ◀2▶

Size K-10.5 (6.5 mm) double-ended crochet hook (or size required to obtain gauge)

Size J-10 (6 mm) crochet hook

Rose Lace Scarf

A: 1 ball of Sevilla from Katia (100% nylon; 153 yds/140 m; 1¾ oz/50 g), color 60 ◀4▶

B: 1 ball of Waikiki from Crystal Palace Yarns (70% rayon, 30% cotton; 105 yds/96 m; 1¾ oz/50 g), color 3001 ◀2▶

Size K-10.5 (6.5 mm) double-ended crochet hook (or size required to obtain gauge)

Size J-10 (6 mm) crochet hook

Gauge

23 sts x 14 rows = 4" using size K-10.5 (6.5 mm) double-ended crochet hook over ripple patt

NOTE: When picking up a loop in horizontal stitch, insert hook under top loop only (see page 15 for instructions on working with a double-ended crochet hook).

Scarf

Row 1: With A and double-ended hook, ch 23, pick up lp in 2nd ch from hook and each additional ch across, keeping all lps on hook. Slide lps to opposite end of hook, turn. [23 lps on hook]

Row 2: To work lps off hook, place B on hook with slip knot, draw slip knot through first 3 lps, *(yo, draw through 2 lps) 3 times, ch 3, (yo, draw through 2 lps) 3 times*, yo, draw through 6 lps, rep from * to * once, yo, draw through 4 lps. Do not turn. [1 lp on hook]

Row 3: With B, ch 1, sk first cl, *(sc lp in next horizontal st) 3 times, (sc lp in ch space) 4 times, (sc lp in next horizontal st) 3 times, sc lp in top of cl*, rep from * to * across. Slide lps to opposite end of hook and turn. [23 lps on hook]

Row 4: Pick up A, yo, draw through 3 lps, *(yo, draw through 2 lps) 3 times, ch 3, (yo, draw through 2 lps) 3 times*, yo, draw through 6 lps, rep from * to * once, yo, draw through 4 lps. Do not turn. [1 lp on hook]

NOTE: The first (yo, draw through 2 lps) after the chain 3 on row 4 creates the fourth chain to work into for row 5.

Row 5: With A, ch 1, sk first cl, *(pick up lp in next horizontal st) 3 times, (pick up lp in next ch) 4 times, (pick up lp in next horizontal st) 3 times, pick up lp in top of cl*, rep from * to * across. Slide lps to opposite end of hook and turn. [23 lps on hook]

Row 6: With B, rep row 4.

Rows 7–164: Rep rows 3–6, ending with row 4. Fasten off B.

Row 165: With A, *(sl st in next horizontal st) 3 times, (sl st in next ch) 4 times, (sl st in next horizontal st) 3 times, sk cl*, rep from * to * across, transfer final lp to standard hook to work edging.

Edging

Using A and standard hook with predominantly B side facing, working in ends of rows, opposite side of foundation ch, and final row as needed, sc evenly around for 1 rnd, working an additional sc in each corner if needed to keep scarf flat. Fasten off. Weave in ends.

Alpaca Beret

By Janet Rehfeldt

Here's an elegant and luxurious beret that will pamper your head and keep you warm at the same time. Made with soft alpaca yarn, the beret features a knitlike cuff of slip stitches. An easy textured check pattern gives a Fair Isle look at the base of the beret, then expands into large stripes. Best of all, the beret is completely reversible.

Skill Level: Easy ◼◼☐☐

Approximate Dimensions

To fit 18"–23" head circumference

Featured Stitches

Back loop (bl)
Chain (ch)
Double crochet (dc)
Single crochet (sc)
Slip stitch (sl st)

Materials

A: 1 ball of 100% Alpaca from Blue Sky Alpacas (100% alpaca; 110 yds; 1.75 oz), color 000 ⓷

B: 1 ball of 100% Alpaca from Blue Sky Alpacas (100% alpaca; 110 yds; 1.75 oz), color 309 ⓷

Size F-5 (3.75 mm) crochet hook

Size G-6 (4.25 mm) crochet hook (or size required to obtain gauge)

12 stitch markers

Gauge

18 sts = 4" in color patt using size G-6 (4.25 mm) crochet hook

Bottom Band

> **NOTE:** *Bottom band is worked sideways. The slip stitches tend to lie at the back of the work. Tilt the work toward you so stitches are easier to see, and work into the correct loop of the slip stitch.*

Row 1: With A and size F-5 hook, ch 7, sl st in 2nd ch from hook, sl st into each ch across, turn. [6 sl sts]

Row 2: Ch 1, sl st in bl only of each sl st across.

Rep row 2 until piece measures approx 17". Do not fasten off.

Beret

> **NOTE:** *Hat is worked in the round. Do not chain 1 at beginning of rounds. Do not join rounds unless otherwise instructed.*

Rnd 1: Working along long edge of band, work 84 sc evenly spaced, sl st to first sc to form a ring and close rnd. Sew short ends of band tog. [84 sc]

Rnd 2: Change to size G-6 hook, *sc in next sc, dc in next sc*, rep from * to * around.

Rnd 3: *Sc in next sc, ch 1, sk next dc*, rep from * to * around.

Rnd 4 (inc rnd): *(Sc in next sc, dc in next ch-1 sp) twice, sc in next sc, (1 sc, 1 dc) in next ch-1 sp*, rep from * to * around. [98 sts]

Rnd 5: *(Sc in next sc, ch 1, sk next dc) twice, (sc in next sc, ch 1) twice, sk next dc*, rep from * to * around. [112 sts]

Rnd 6: *Sc in next sc, dc in next ch-1 sp*, rep from * to * around.

Rnd 7: *(Sc in next sc, ch 1, sk next dc) 7 times, sc in next sc, ch 1, sc in next dc, ch 1*, rep from * to * around. [126 sts]

Rnd 8: Sc in next sc, dc in next ch-1 sp*, rep from * to * around.

Rnd 9: *(Sc in next sc, ch 1, sk next dc) 8 times, sc in next sc, ch 1, sc in next dc, ch 1*, rep from * to * around. [140 sts]

Rnd 10: *Sc in next sc, dc in next ch-1 sp*, rep from * to * around. Do not cut A. [142 sts]

Rnd 11: Change to B, *sc in next sc, ch 1, sk next dc*, rep from * to * around. Do not cut B.

Rnd 12: Change to A, *sc in next sc, dc in ch-1 sp*, rep from * to * around. Do not cut A.

Rnds 13–16: Rep rnds 11 and 12 twice. At end of rnd 16, cut A, leaving a 6" tail.

Rnd 17: Change to B, *sc in next sc, ch 1, sk next dc*, rep from * to * around.

Rnd 18: *Sc in next sc, dc in ch-1 sp*, rep from * to *around.

Rnd 19: *Sc in next sc, ch 1, sk next dc*, rep from * to * around.

Rnd 20 (dec rnd): *(Sc in next sc, dc in next ch-1 sp) 6 times, sc2tog over next sc and ch-1 sp*, rep from * to * around. [130 sts]

Rnd 21: *(Sc in next sc, ch 1, sk next dc) 6 times, sc in next sc*, rep from * to * around.

Rnd 22: (Sc in next sc, dc in next ch-1 sp) 6 times, sc2tog over next 2 sc, dc in next ch-1 sp, *(sc in next sc, dc in next ch-1 sp) 5 times, sc2tog over next 2 sc, dc in next ch-1 sp*, rep from * to * around, on last rep, sk last sc of prev rnd. [120 sts]

Rnd 23: Rep rnd 19.

Rnd 24: *(Sc in next sc, dc in next ch-1 sp) 5 times, sc2tog over next sc and ch-1 sp*, rep from * to * around. [110 sts]

Rnd 25: *(Sc in next sc, ch 1, sk next dc) 5 times, sc in next sc*, rep from * to * around.

Rnd 26: (Sc in next sc, dc in next ch-1 sp) 5 times, sc2tog over next 2 sc, dc in next ch-1 sp, *(sc in next sc, dc in next ch-1 sp) 4 times, sc2tog over next 2 sc, dc in next ch-1 sp*, rep from * to * around, on last rep, sk last sc of prev rnd. Cut B, leaving a 6" tail. [100 sts]

Rnd 27: Change to A and rep rnd 19.

Rnd 28: *(Sc in next sc, dc in next ch-1 sp) 4 times, sc2tog over next sc and ch-1 sp*, rep from * to * around. [90 sts]

Rnd 29: *(Sc in next sc, ch 1, sk next dc) 4 times, sc in next sc*, rep from * to * around.

Rnd 30: (Sc in next sc, dc in next ch-1 sp) 4 times, sc2tog over next 2 sc, dc in next ch-1 sp, *(sc in next sc, dc in next ch-1 sp) 3 times, sc2tog over next 2 sc, dc in next ch-1 sp*, rep from * to *around, on last rep, sk last sc of prev rnd. Cut A, leaving a 6" tail. [80 sts]

Rnd 31: Change to B and rep rnd 19.

Rnd 32: *(Sc in next sc, dc in next ch-1 sp) 3 times, sc2tog over next sc and ch-1 sp*, rep from * to * around. [70 sts]

Rnd 33: (Sc in next sc, ch 1, sk next dc) 3 times, sc2tog over next 2 sc, ch 1, sk next dc, *(sc in next sc, ch 1, sk next dc) twice, sc2tog over next 2 sc, ch 1, sk next dc*, rep from * to * around, on last rep, sk last sc of prev rnd. [60 sts]

Rnd 34: *(Sc in next sc, dc in next ch-1 sp) 3 times, sc2tog over next sc and ch-1 sp*, rep from * to * around. [50 sts]

Rnd 35: (Sc in next sc, ch 1, sk next dc) twice, sc2tog over next 2 sc, ch 1, sk next dc, *sc in next sc, ch 1, sk next dc, sc2tog over next 2 sc, ch 1, sk next dc*, rep from * to * around to last 3 sts, sc2tog over next sc and dc, ch 1, sk last sc of prev rnd. [40 sts]

Rnd 36: *(Sc in next sc, dc in next ch-1 sp), sc2tog over next sc and ch-1 sp*, rep from * to * around. [30 sts]

Rnd 37: *Sc in next sc, sc2tog over next 2 sts*, rep from * to * around. [20 sts]

Rnds 38 and 39: Sc2tog around. [5 sts]

Fasten off, leaving a 6" tail. Thread tail through last rnd of sts and pull closed. Weave in ends.

Pull-Up Pinkies

By Janet Rehfeldt and Carol Lykins

These Pull-Up Pinkies are the perfect mitten-and-glove combination. Pull up the attached mitten section over the short-fingered gloves to keep your fingers toasty and warm. Then push them off and to the back of the hand when you need to be able to use your fingers freely. For working in a chilly office, make the short-fingered gloves without the pull-up section.

Skill Level: Experienced ■■■■

Approximate Dimensions

Small (Medium, Large) to fit 6¾ (7¼, 8)" hand circumference

Featured Stitches

Back loop (bl)
Chain (ch)
Single crochet (sc)
Slip stitch (sl st)

Materials

2 (2, 2) balls of Dalegarn Baby Ull from Dale of Norway (100% wool; 175 m; 50 g), color 4018 (2)

OR

2 (3, 3) balls of Regia 4-ply, 6-color from Schachenmayr Nomotta (75% new wool, 25% polyamide; 125 m; 50 g), color 5033 (2)

Size C-2 (2.75 mm) crochet hook

Size D-3 (3.25 mm) crochet hook (or size required to obtain gauge)

2 stitch markers

Gauge

14.5 sc x 13 rows= 2" using size D-3 (3.25 mm) crochet hook

Left Mitten

Cuff

> **NOTE:** *Cuff is worked sideways.*

Row 1: With size C-2 hook, ch 11, working in the bottom hump, sc in 2nd ch from hook, sc in each ch, turn.

Row 2: Ch 1, bl sc in first sc, bl sc in each sc, turn. [10 sc]

Rows 3–40 (44, 48): Rep row 2.

Hand

> **NOTE:** *Hand section is worked in the round. Count chains as stitches unless otherwise instructed.*

Rnd 1: Change to size D-3 hook, working along long edge of cuff, evenly sc 46 (52, 58) sts, sl st in first sc to form a circle and close ring. Sew seam along short edge of cuff.

Rnd 2: Sc in first sc, ch 1, sk 1 sc, *sc in next sc, ch 1, sk 1 sc*, rep from * to * around. Pm in first sc of rnd to mark beg of rnds. [46 (52, 58) sts]

Rnd 3: *Sc in next sc, ch 1, sk next ch-1 sp*, rep from * to * around.

Rep rnd 3 until piece measures 1" above cuff.

Thumb Gusset

Rnd 1 (inc rnd): (Sc in next sc, ch 1, sk next ch-1 sp) twice, sc in next ch-1 sp, move beg rnd marker to sc just completed, ch 1, sc in next sc, ch 1, sc in next ch-1 sp, pm in sc just completed, ch 1, *sc in next sc, ch 1, sk next ch-1 sp*, rep from * to * around. [50 (56, 62) sts]

Rnd 2: *Sc in next sc, ch 1, sk next ch-1 sp*, rep from * to * around. Move markers with each rnd as instructed.

Rnd 3: Sc in sc with marker, move marker to sc just completed, ch 1, sc in next ch-1 sp, ch 1, work in patt to ch-1 sp before next marker, sc in next ch-1 sp, ch 1, sc in sc with marker, move marker to sc just completed, ch 1, *sc in next sc, ch 1, sk next ch-1 sp*, rep from * to * around. [54 (60, 66) sts]

Rep rnds 2 and 3 another 4 (5, 6) times. Then rep rnd 2 once more. [70 (80, 90) sts]

Next rnd: Sc in next sc, ch 1, sk next ch-1 sp, sk next 24 (28, 32) sts, *sc in next sc, ch, 1, sk next ch-1 sp*, rep from * to * around. Remove markers. [46 (52, 58) sts]

Next rnd: *Sc in next sc, pm to mark new beg of rnds, ch 1, sk next ch-1 sp*, rep from * to * around.

Rep last rnd 3 (3, 4) times, moving marker with each rnd.

Pull-Up Mitten Section

Fold mitten in half so thumb opening is on palm, with edge of thumb 2 sc sts from side edge of mitten. Work in patt to right edge of mitten where little finger would be located and with palm side facing you.

Rnd 1: Sc in next sc, ch 1, sk next ch-1 sp, ch 23 (25, 28), sk center 20 (24, 28) sts and ch sp on glove palm, *sc in next sc, ch 1, sk next ch-1 sp, pm in skipped ch-1 sp*, rep from * to * around to beg of ch 23 (25, 28). Pm in last skipped ch-1 sp. Leave markers in place to mark glove-finger section.

Rnd 2: Sc in each ch along ch 23 (25, 28), *sc in next sc, ch 1, sk next ch-1 sp*, rep from * to * around.

Rnd 3: Leave sc lp unworked and at front of work, working behind sc lp and into hand section only, *sc in next sc on hand section, ch 1, sk next ch-1 sp on hand*, rep from * to * along front part of hand. Working into ch-1 sp with markers and folding rnd 2 down to front of work, sc in first ch-1 sp, ch 1, **sc in next ch-1 sp, ch 1**, rep from ** to **, working into each marked ch-1 sp and removing markers. [46 (52, 58) sts]

Leave rnd 3 to inside of work to use later for glove section.

Rnd 4: Working in rnd 2 of mitten section, (sc in next sc, ch 1, sk next sc) 11 (12, 12) times, *sc in next sc, ch 1, sk next ch-1 sp*, rep from * to * on rem sts. [50 (54, 60) sts]

Rnd 5: *Sc in next sc, ch 1, sk next ch-1 sp*, rep from * to * around. Move markers with each rnd.

Rep rnd 5 until mitten measures 6 (6½, 7)" above cuff or just to tip of little finger.

Top Shaping

To dec when instructed: Insert hook into next sc, yo, pull up lp, insert hook into next ch-1 sp, yo, pull up lp, yo, pull through 2 lps on hook, insert hook into next sc, yo, pull up lp, yo, pull through 3 lps on hook—3-st dec made.

Rnd 1 (dec rnd): *Sc in next sc, ch 1, sk next ch-1 sp (4, 3, 5) times, dec over next 3 sts, ch 1*, rep from * to * around to last 2 (4, 4) sts, sc in next sc, ch 1, sk next ch-1 sp in last 2 (4, 4) sts. [42 (44, 52) sts]

Rnd 2: *Sc in next sc, ch 1, sk next ch-1 sp*, rep from * to * around.

Rnd 3: *Sc in next sc, ch 1, sk next ch-1 sp (3, 3, 4) times, dec over next 3 sts, ch 1*, rep from * to * around to last 2 (4, 4) sts, sc in next sc, ch 1, sk next ch-1 sp in last 2 (4, 4) sts. [34 (36, 44) sts]

Rnd 4: Rep rnd 2.

Rnd 5: *Sc in next sc, ch 1, sk next ch-1 sp (3, 4, 3) times, dec over next 3 sts, ch 1*, rep from * to * around to last 4 (0, 4) sts, sc in next sc, ch 1, sk next ch-1 sp in last 4 (0, 4) sts. [28 (30, 36) sts]

Rnd 6: Rep rnd 2.

Rnd 7: *Sc in next sc, ch 1, sk next ch-1 sp (4, 3, 2) times, dec over next 3 sts, ch 1*, rep from * to * around to last 4 (0, 4) sts, sc in next sc, ch 1, sk next ch-1 sp in last 4 (0, 4) sts. [24 (24, 28) sts]

Rnd 8: Rep rnd 2.

Rnd 9: *Sc in next sc, ch 1, sk next ch-1 sp (2, 2, 2) times, dec over next 3 sts, ch 1*, rep from * to * around, sl st in first sc to close rnd. [18 (18, 22) sts]

Fasten off, leaving a 6" tail. Weave tail through last rnd and pull tight to close top of mitten. Anchor with a sewing stitch.

Glove Section

Fold mitten section back and out of the way. Working in rnd 3 from pull-up mitten section, attach yarn to sc at right edge on back of hand with a sl st.

Rnd 1: Sc in same sc as join, ch 1, sk next ch-1 sp, *sc in next sc, ch 1, sk next ch-1 sp*, rep from * to * around. [46 (52, 58) sts]

Rnd 2: *Sc in next sc, ch 1, sk next ch-1 sp*, rep from * to * around.

Rep rnd 2 an additional 2 (3, 4) times. Do not fasten off.

> *NOTE: To begin fingers, work stitches on the palm as indicated, then skip the rest of the hand, chain 2, and work the number of stitches indicated on the back of the hand.*

Little Finger

Rnd 1: Work to side edge at little finger with back of hand facing you, and 6 sts rem to side edge of hand. (Sc in next sc, ch 1, sk next ch-1 sp) 6 times, ch 2. Pm in first sc to mark beg of rnds. [14 (14, 14) sts]

Rnd 2: (Sc in next sc, ch 1, sk next ch-1 sp) 6 times, (sc, ch 1 into next ch st of ch-2 sts) 2 (2, 3) times. [16 (16, 18) sts]

Rnd 3: *Sc in next sc, ch 1, sk next ch-1 sp*, rep from * to * around.

Rep rnd 3 an additional 2 (3, 3) times or until just below first knuckle on finger. Sl st to first sc, fasten off.

Ring Finger

Leaving a 6" tail, attach yarn on palm side of glove into sc at base of little finger on palm (not ch-2 sts between fingers) in rnd 1 of little finger.

Rnd 1: Sc in same st as join, ch 1, sk next ch-1 sp, *(sc in next sc, ch 1, sk next ch-1 sp) 3 (3, 4) times*, ch 2. Working in corresponding sts on opposite side, count 6 (6, 8) sts away from little finger and rep from * to * once, working in base of sts in ch 2 of rnd 1, (sc, ch 1) between next 2 sc. [8 (8, 10) sc, 10 (10, 12) ch]

Rnd 2: (Sc in next sc, ch 1, sk next ch-1 sp) 4 (4, 5) times, (sc, ch 1 into next ch st) twice, (sc in next sc, ch 1, sk next ch-1 sp) 3 (4, 4) times, pm to mark beg of rnd. [20 (20, 24) sts]

Rnd 3: *Sc in next sc, ch 1, sk next ch-1 sp*, rep from * to * around.

Rep rnd 3 an additional 2 (3, 3) times or until just below first knuckle on finger. Sl st to first sc, fasten off.

Middle Finger

Leaving a 6" tail, attach yarn on palm side of glove into sc at base of last finger on palm (not ch-2 sts between fingers) in rnd 1 of last finger.

Rnd 1: Sc in same st as join, ch 1, sk next ch-1 sp, *(sc in next sc, ch 1, sk next ch-1 sp) 3 (3, 4) times*, ch 2. Working in corresponding sts on opposite side, count 6 (6, 8) sts away from last finger, rep from * to * once, working in base of sts in ch 2 of rnd 1, (sc, ch 1) between next 2 sc. [8 (8, 10) sc, 10 (10, 12) ch]

Rep rem instructions for ring finger.

Forefinger

Leaving a 6" tail, attach yarn on palm side of glove into sc at base of last finger on palm (not ch-2 sts between fingers) in rnd 1 of middle finger.

Rnd 1: Sc in same st as join, ch 1, sk next ch-1 sp, (sc in next sc, ch 1, sk next ch-1 sp) 7 (8, 8) times, (sc, ch 1) in base of sc of rnd 1 of last finger 0 (0, 1) times, working in base of sts of ch 2 on rnd 1, (sc, ch 1) twice. [20 (22, 24) sts]

Rnd 2: *Sc in next sc, ch 1, sk next ch-1 sp*, rep from * to * around.

Rep rnd 2 an additional 3 (4, 4) times or until just below first knuckle on finger. Sl st to first sc, fasten off.

Thumb

Rnd 1: Leaving a 6" tail, attach yarn to first sc of thumb-gusset opening on palm side. Sc in same st as join, ch 1, (sc in next sc, ch 1, sk next ch-1 sp) 12 (14, 16) times. [24 (28, 32) sts]

Rnd 2: To close gap at thumb, working in base of sts on hand at thumb-gusset join, insert hook into base of sc, yo, pull up lp, insert hook into first sc of rnd 1 of thumb, yo, pull up lp, yo, pull through 3 lps on hook (counts as first sc of rnd), ch 1, *sc in next sc, ch 1, sk next ch-1 sp*, rep from * to * around. [24 (28, 32) sts]

Rnd 3: *Sc in next sc, ch 1, sk next ch-1 sp*, rep from * to * around.

Rnd 4 (dec rnd): Dec over next 3 sts, *sc in next sc, ch 1, sk next ch-1 sp*, rep from * to * around. [22 (26, 30) sts]

Rnd 5: Rep rnd 3.

Rnd 6: Dec over next 3 sts, *sc in next sc, ch 1, sk next ch-1 sp*, rep from * to * around. [20 (24, 28) sc]

Rep rnd 3 until ¼" shorter than length of thumb, do not fasten off.

Next rnd (dec rnd): Dec over next 3 sts, *(sc in next sc, ch 1, sk next ch-1 sp), dec over next 3 sts*, rep from * to * to last 2 (0, 4) sts, sc in next sc, ch 1, sk next ch-1 sp) 1 (0, 2) time. [16 (16, 22) sts]

Next rnd: *Sc, in next sc, ch 1, sk next ch-1 sp*, rep from * to * around.

Next rnd: Sc in each sc, skipping all ch-1 spaces. [8 (8, 11) sts]

Last rnd: Sc in each sc.

Fasten off, leaving a 6" tail. Weave tail through last rnd and pull tight to close top of mitten. Anchor with a sewing stitch. Weave in ends, sewing closed any gaps at base of fingers and thumb.

Right Hand

Work as for left hand to pull-up mitten section.

Pull-Up Mitten Section

Fold mitten in half so that right edge of thumb-gusset section is located 2 sc sts before the right edge of mitten. You do not want the beginning of the thumb gusset at the very edge of the work. Work to left edge of mitten where thumb would be located and with palm side facing you. Continue with remaining instructions to fingers.

Little Finger

Rnd 1: Work to side edge at little finger with palm of hand facing you to within 6 (6, 6) sts, (sc in next sc, ch 1, sk next ch-1 sp) 6 times, ch 2. [6 (6, 6) sc, 8 (8, 8) ch]

Cont with rem instructions for finger and thumb portion of mittens, reversing join to hand side of glove. Fasten off and weave in ends.

Short-Fingered Gloves

Follow instructions for "Pull-Up Mitten Section." Cont working on [46 (52, 58) sts] until glove reaches base of little finger. Work finger sections of glove as instructed.

Work rnds 1–6 of thumb. Then rep rnd 3 an additional 2 (3, 3) times or until just below first knuckle on thumb.

Next rnd: (Sc in next sc, ch 1, sk next ch-1 sp), *sc in next sc, (sc in next sc, ch 1, sk next ch-1 sp)*, rep from * to * around, fasten off. Weave in ends, sewing closed any gaps at base of fingers and thumb.

Short-fingered gloves

Star-Stitch Belt

By Nancy Nehring

This belt can be made from any small, smooth, stiff thread or cord. Examples are shown in linen, gimp, and leather string. Simple buckles are available at a fabric store, but to find a more unusual buckle, try flea markets, arts-and-crafts fairs, or vintage fashion shops.

Skill Level: Intermediate ◼◼◼◻

Approximate Dimensions

Custom sizing: Width needed to fit your buckle, length needed for your waist.

Featured Stitch

Chain (ch)

Special Stitch

Star stitch (see project instructions)

> **NOTE:** *The amount of thread or cord you need depends on the thickness, stiffness, width, and length you want your belt. A belt 1½" wide and 28" long will take about 100 yards. Make a swatch to determine how much thread or cord you need. If you've never worked with leather before, see "Crocheting with Leather" on page 8.*

Materials

1 ball of 16/4 Henry's Attic Normandy linen (100% linen; 1200 yds; 16 oz), color Natural 🔗

Size 5 (1.70 mm) steel crochet hook

OR

1 ball of size #3 gimp cording, color Blue 🔗

Size 00 (2.70 mm) steel crochet hook

OR

120 yds of ½-mm-diameter leather string, color Black 🔗

Size 1 (2.25 mm) steel hook

Buckle

Yarn needle

Gauge

Linen: 5 star stitches x 4 rows = 1" using size 5 (1.70 mm) steel hook

Gimp: 1½ star stitches x 4 rows = 1" using size 00 (2.70 mm) steel hook

Leather string: 4 star stitches x 2 rows = 1" using size 1 (2.25 mm) steel hook

Your thread or cord may produce a different gauge, but you must work tightly so that the star pattern shows.

Belt

> **NOTE:** *Belt is worked from side to side.*

Measure the length of the bar on your buckle. This is the width that you'll make your belt before adding the edge finish. Cut a length of thread or cord 2 times the belt length plus 12". Set aside.

Chain an even number of stitches as needed for the length of your belt plus ⅓ more (chain gets smaller as first row of star stitches is made) plus enough stitches for 1" (to attach belt to buckle). For example, for a 24" waist, ch 24" for waist size plus 8" for an additional ⅓, plus 1" for attaching belt to buckle—33" total length.

Row 1: Yo, insert hook in 2nd ch from hook, pull through, yo, insert hook in next ch, pull through, yo, sk 1 ch, insert hook in next ch, pull through, yo and pull through all 7 lps on hook, ch 1 (this forms an "eye" in the center of the stitch); *yo, insert hook in eye just made, pull through, yo, insert hook in same ch as last ch of foundation row used, pull through, yo, sk 1 ch, insert hook in next ch, pull through, yo and pull through all 7 lps on hook, ch 1*, rep from * to * to end of row, turn.

> **NOTE:** *If the belt isn't the right size or is just slightly too long after the first row of star stitches is complete, rip back to the beginning chain and adjust as necessary.*

Row 2: Ch 3, yo, insert hook in 2nd ch from hook, pull through, yo, insert hook in last eye of previous row, pull through, yo, insert hook in next eye, pull through, yo and pull through all 7 lps on hook, ch 1, *yo, insert hook in eye just made, pull through, yo, insert hook in eye of previous row used in last st made, pull through, yo, insert hook in next eye of previous row, pull through, yo and pull through all 7 lps on hook, ch 1*, rep from * to * to end of row, turn.

Rep row 2 until belt is same width as bar on buckle.

Edge Finish

Work 2 sc in each end row or star stitch over reserved length of thread or cord around entire edge. Pull up ends of reserved thread or cord to adjust and stabilize length of belt. For a stiffer edge, you can work over multiple lengths of thread or cord. Sew one end of belt around bar of buckle, using the same thread or cord.

Crossed-Stitch Belt

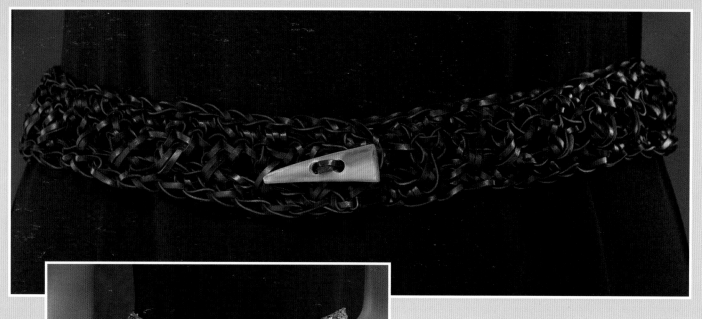

By Janet Rehfeldt

This terrific belt can be crocheted using leather lacing, ribbon, or faux suede. The finishing can be a sophisticated button, such as the horn that was used in the model, or you can leave long strands that loop over each other or tie, making the design very versatile. Both the ribbon and the leather stretch to accommodate several sizes.

Skill Level: Easy ◼◼◻◻

Approximate Dimensions

Leather belt: 1¾" wide x 26½ (32, 37¼)" long

Ribbon belt: 1½" wide x 26½ (32, 37¼)" long

Featured Stitches

Chain (ch)
Crossed stitch, page 16
Double crochet (dc)
Half double crochet (hdc)
Single crochet (sc)

Materials

Leather Belt

1 spool of ⅛"-wide flat leather lacing from Tejas Lace (smooth leather; 50 yds) color 502202 (4)

Size L-11 (8 mm) crochet hook (or size required to obtain gauge)

1 natural horn-shaped button, 1¼"

Ribbon Belt

1 ball of Zen Color from Berroco (55% cotton, 45% nylon; 110 yds/102 m; 1.75 oz/50 g), color 8026 (4)

OR

1 ball of Suede from Berroco (100% nylon; 1.75 oz/50 g; 120 yds/111 m), color 3745 (4)

Size L-11 (8 mm) crochet hook (or size required to obtain gauge)

6 wooden beads, ½" (optional)

Gauge

4½ cross sts = 4" using size L-11 (8 mm) crochet hook

> **NOTE:** *Leather lacing and ribbon both stretch. If you've never worked with leather or ribbon before, see "Crocheting with Leather" on page 8 and "Ribbons" on page 7.*

Belt

Row 1: Ch 63 (75, 87), working in bottom hump of ch, sc in 2nd ch from hook, sc in each ch across, turn. [62 (74, 86) sc]

Row 2: Ch 2, hdc in first sc, *sk 1 sc, dc in next sc, dc in skipped sc*, rep from * to * across to last sc, hdc in last sc, turn. [30 (36, 42) cross sts]

Row 3: Ch 1, sc in first st, sc in each st across, do not turn. Pivot work to work along short side edge, work 3 sc along side edge.

Fasten off, leaving a 6" tail. Weave in ends. Sew button at one end or attach fringe.

Fringe (Optional)

Cut eight 28" strands. Fold 1 strand in half to form a lp, insert crochet hook through back of work to front, place lp onto hook, draw lp through piece, then bring ends through lp and tighten. Evenly space 4 fringes along each end of belt. Attach beads to 3 strands on each end by slipping bead up onto strand, then knotting strand below bead.

So Very Chic Headband

By Janet Rehfeldt

You'll be so very chic wearing this headband crocheted in ribbon or faux suede and embellished with a small chain or strand of beads.

Skill Level: Easy ◼◼▢▢

Approximate Dimensions

To fit 18"–23" head circumference

Approx finished length: 18½"

Featured Stitches

Chain (ch)
Crossed stitch, page 16
Double crochet (dc)
Single crochet (sc)

Materials

1 ball of Suede from Berroco (100% nylon; 120 yds/111 m; 1.75 oz/50 g), color 3717 ◖4◗

OR

1 ball of Glacé from Berroco (100% rayon; 75 yds/69 m; 1.75 oz/50 g), color 2012 ◖4◗

OR

1 ball of Zodiac from Berroco (53% cotton, 47% nylon; 97 yds/90 m; 1.75 oz/50 g), color 9635 ◖4◗

Size E-4 (3.5 mm) crochet hook (or size required to obtain gauge)

30" metal chain with small links

OR

190 size 6/0 E beads and dental floss for stringing beads

Sewing thread to match yarn color

Gauge

7 crossed sts = 4" using size E-4 (3.5 mm) crochet hook

Headband

Rnd 1: Ch 82, working in bottom hump of ch, sc in 2nd ch from hook, sc in each ch across, sl st to first sc to form a circle and close rnd. [81 sc]

Rnd 2: Ch 1, dc in first sc, sk next sc, dc in next sc, ch 1, dc in skipped sc, *sk next sc, dc in next sc, ch 1, dc in skipped sc*, rep from * to * around, sl st to top of first dc. [40 crossed sts plus 1 dc]

Rnd 3: Ch 2 (counts as first dc of this rnd), sk first 2 dc and ch-1 sp, dc in next dc, ch 1, dc in skipped dc, *sk next ch-1 sp and dc, dc in next dc, ch 1, dc in skipped dc* (crossed sts should be slightly offset from sts in rnd 2), rep from * to * around, sl st to top of beg ch 2.

Rnd 4: Ch 1, sc in each dc around, skipping all ch-1 spaces. [81 sc]

Fasten off.

Chain Embellishment (Optional)

Sk first 2 crossed sts from beg of rnd 2, attach metal ch to right side with a sewing st to 2nd dc of next crossed st in rnd 2. Thread metal ch around base of next st from front to back to front again, working ch through top lp of sc from rnd 1 and then under post of dc st and up between cross; take ch up to rnd 3, skipping crossed sts; thread ch around next st, going from front to back to front; make sure ch is caught above a st strand and not just wrapped around post or it will slide down and will not keep a nice diagonal track when headband is on your head.

Cont to thread ch through crossed sts between the 2 rnds, stopping just before 3 crossed sts from end of rnd. On wrong side of headband, ch should only show around base of 1 st; it should not strand over multiple sts. Have 3 crossed sts between each metal ch on both upper and lower rows (see photo of headband).

Bead Embellishment (Optional)

String beads onto about 30" of a strong thread or dental floss (see page 10). Sk first 2 crossed sts from beg of rnd 2, attach thread to headband on underside and secure. Bring strand up to right side of headband and follow instructions for stranding chain through headband. Try not to have many beads go to the wrong side of the headband or it will be uncomfortable to wear.

Easy Suede Headband

by Janet Rehfeldt

This project is fast and easy. The headband can be sized to fit most anyone, making this the perfect fast gift item. The suede leather lacing in neutral or bright colors is so fashionable that this accessory works for either a casual or dressy day.

Skill Level: Easy ◖■□▷

Approximate Dimensions

To fit 16"–26" head circumference

Headband is adjusted to fit the head of the person. Each headband will be different.

Featured Stitches

Chain (ch)
Single crochet (sc)

Materials

1 spool of ⅛"-wide suede lacing from Tejas Lace (100% cut rawhide suede; 25 yds), color 5020-50, 5014-08, or 5014-07 ⬤⑤

Size K-10.5 (6.5 mm) crochet hook

Gauge

8.5 sc = 4" using size K-10.5 (6.5 mm) crochet hook

> **NOTE:** *If you've never worked with leather before, see "Crocheting with Leather" on page 8.*

Headband

Row 1: Leaving a 12" tail, ch 30 (36). Working in bottom hump of chain, sc in 2nd ch from hook, *sc in next ch*, rep from * to * across. Fasten off, leaving a 12" tail. [29 (35) sc]

Place headband on head, holding tails at one end against opposite end of headband and marking tails at point where headband fits comfortably. Pull tails through opposite end of headband to form a circle, stopping at marker point. Weave ends into work under several sts, then wrap around a strand of leather by going under strand, over strand, and under the same strand to form a kind of wrapped knot to secure woven strands, then weave under several more sts.

Textured Watchband and Anklet

By Janet Rehfeldt

Using leather jeweler's cord is a great way to add a new band to either an old watch that has been stashed away in your jewelry box or a new purchased watch face. The leather cording is easy to use and creates a wonderfully textured pattern for the watchband. The anklet is one of today's hot accessories no matter what your age and it is the perfect complement to the watchband. For a different look, try wire and beads.

Skill Level

Leather Band: Easy ◖◼◻◗

Wire Beaded Band: Experienced ◖◼◼◗

Approximate Dimensions

Watchband: 6½ (7½, 8½)" circumference (including watch face)

Anklet: 7½ (9, 11)" circumference

Featured Stitches

Beaded slip stitch (beaded sl st), page 11
Chain (ch)
Double crochet (dc)
Slip stitch (sl st)

Materials

Leather Watchband

1 spool of Jewelry Designer leather cord from Darice (1-mm diameter, 3 yds), color 1919-02 black

Size D-3 (3.25 mm) crochet hook (or size required to obtain gauge)

1 Crystal Innovations Designer watch face, 1" silver rectangle with ring attachment

1 clasp, ⅜"

Fabric glue (optional)

Beaded Watchband

1 spool of craft wire from Darice (26 gauge, 40 yds), color 39580-73 dark blue **①**

Size D-3 (3.25 mm) crochet hook (or size required to obtain gauge)

12 size 6/0 E beads

1 Crystal Innovations Designer watch face, 1" silver oval with ring attachment

1 clasp, ⅜"

2 crimp tubes (optional)

Leather Anklet

2 spools of Jewelry Designer leather cord from Darice (1-mm diameter, 3 yds), color 1919-02 black

Size D-3 (3.25 mm) crochet hook (or size required to obtain gauge)

1 clasp, ⅜"

Fabric glue (optional)

Beaded Anklet

1 spool of craft wire from Darice (26 gauge, 40 yds), color 39580-73 dark blue **①**

Size D-3 (3.25 mm) crochet hook (or size required to obtain gauge)

26 (30, 36) size 6/0 E beads

1 clasp, ⅜"

2 crimp tubes (optional)

> **NOTE:** One spool of wire will make both the watchband and anklet.

Gauge

6.5 sts = 1" using size D-3 (3.25 mm) crochet hook over patt st

> **NOTE:** If you've never worked with leather or wire before, see "Crocheting with Leather" on page 8 and "Crocheting with Wire" on page 9.

Leather Watchband

Leaving a 5" tail, ch 12 (14, 16). Sl st to watch face, turn. Working in bottom hump of ch, sl st in next ch from hook, dc in next ch, *sl st in next ch, dc in next

ch*, rep from * to * across. Fasten off, leaving a 5" tail. Rep for second side of watch.

Finishing

Attach bracelet clasp to each end as follows: Slip one tail end into ring of clasp in one direction, slip other tail end into clasp in other direction; with tapestry needle, weave one leather end into bracelet, making sure to wrap around a single strand of leather by going under the strand, over the top, and back under it again (this creates a kind of wrapped knot), then *go under multiple strands, then around another single strand*, rep from * to * several times. Weave second tail.

Rep for opposite side. When done, if desired, dab a tiny drop of fabric glue on tail end on underside of band to keep it secured.

Leather Anklet

String one end of clasp onto leather, ch 50 (60, 72), working in bottom hump of ch, bring clasp up to hook, sl st in 2nd ch from hook, *dc in next ch, sl st in next ch*, rep from * to * across row. [49 (59, 71) sts]

Fasten off. Attach opposite end of clasp, following instructions for finishing watchband.

Beaded Watchband

String beads onto wire (see page 10). Follow instructions for Leather Watchband, working a beaded sl st for each regular sl st and working into 1 lp only of chain. Fasten off, leaving a 6" tail.

To attach the clasp, use the wire to wrap through ring of clasp, thread wire through band, then through ring of clasp again; thread wire into band, cut close, and crimp to band with pliers so that wire won't poke you. Or, before attaching clasp, put a crimp tube onto wire tails, thread wire through ring on clasp, then down into crimp tube. Cut wire close to crimp tube, crimp tube down with pliers onto wire.

Wire Beaded Anklet

String beads onto wire (see page 10). Follow instructions for Leather Anklet, working a beaded sl st for each regular sl st and working into 1 lp only of ch. Fasten off, leaving a 6" tail. Follow instructions for Beaded Watchband to attach clasps.

Teeny-Tiny Sock Earrings

By Mary Jane Wood

These darling Teeny-Tiny Sock Earrings are bound to be a conversation piece. The models were worked in hand-dyed cotton for a one-of-a-kind accessory. A small bead at the base of the earring clasp adds a little more pizzazz.

Skill Level: Intermediate ◼◼◼◻

Approximate Dimensions

¾" circumference x 1" tall

Featured Stitches

Chain (ch)
Single crochet (sc)
Slip stitch (sl st)

Materials

1 skein of Wildflowers embroidery thread from Caron Color (100% cotton; 7 yds), color 070 or 018 🄰

Size 12 (1 mm) steel crochet hook (or size required to obtain gauge)

2 stitch markers

2 fishhook earrings for pierced ears or clip earrings with a gold ring in front

2 small beads (optional)

Pliers

Gauge

10 sc = ¾" using size 12 (1 mm) steel crochet hook

Sock (Make 2)

> **NOTE:** *"Socks" are worked toe to cuff in the round with a short row heel. Do not chain 1 at beginning of rounds. Do not join rounds unless otherwise instructed.*

Toe and Foot

Rnd 1: Ch 5, working in bottom hump, sc in bottom hump of 2nd ch from hook and each of next 3 ch. Pivot work to work in top lps of beg ch, sc in each of 4 ch. [8 sc]

Rnd 2 (inc rnd): Work 2 sc in next st, sc in next 3 sts, 2 sc in next st, sc in rem sts. [10 sc]

Rnds 3–5: Sc in each st. [10 sc]

Heel

> **NOTE:** *Do not chain 1 at beginning of rows unless otherwise instructed.*

Fold sock so toe lies flat, pm at each edge to mark side edges of sock. Work to closest side if not already there.

Row 1 (RS): Sc in each of next 5 sts, leaving rem sts unworked, turn. [5 sc]

Row 2: Sc in each of next 5 sts, turn. [5 sc]

Row 3 (dec row): Sc in first st, sc in each sc to last st, sk last st, turn. Pm in unworked st. [4 sc]

Row 4: Rep row 3, adding a 2nd marker. [3 sc]

Row 5 (inc row): Sc in each st in last row, sc in unworked st, remove marker, sl st in next st on foot, turn. [4 sc]

Row 6: Sk sl st, sc in each st in last row, sc in unworked st, remove marker, sl st in next st on foot, turn. [5 sc]

Leg and Cuff

> **NOTE:** *Do not chain 1 at beginning of rounds. Do not join rounds unless otherwise instructed.*

Rnd 1: With RS facing, sc in next 5 sts on heel, sc in sl st and in next 5 sts on foot. [11 sc]

Rnds 2–7: Sc in each st.

Fasten off and weave in ends. Fold each sock in half and pull into shape. Push bead onto open ring on earring holder. Thread open ring on earring holder through back of stocking. Using pliers, squeeze ring closed.

Beaded Lace Choker

By Janet Rehfeldt

Delicate wire loops and swirls create a unique and beautiful choker. Wire can be molded to create larger or smaller loops in the stitches, giving each choker you make a slightly different look. Don't want to work with wire? Try using size 10 cotton thread or fine metallic thread instead.

Skill Level: Intermediate ◼◼◼▭

Approximate Dimensions

13 (15, 17)" circumference

Featured Stitches

Bead single crochet (bsc), page 11
Chain (ch)
Double crochet (dc)
Single crochet (sc)

Materials

1 spool of craft designer wire from Darice (26 gauge, 40 yds/36.5 m), color 3958-67 🎨

OR

1 skein of Cebelia, size 10, from DMC (100% cotton; 260 m; 50 g), color 223 🎨

Size B-2 (2.25 mm) crochet hook (or size required to obtain gauge)

8 (9, 10) size 6/0 E beads

1 necklace clasp

Small needle-nose pliers

Gauge

23 sc = 4"

> **NOTE:** *If you've never worked with wire before, see "Crocheting with Wire" on page 9.*

Choker

String 9 beads and both ends of clasp onto wire or thread (see page 10).

> **NOTE:** *If using Cebelia from DMC in place of wire, work chain loosely but not sloppily. To have length come out to correct size, make sure to obtain correct gauge.*

Row 1 (RS): Ch 75 (85, 95), sc in 2nd ch from hook as follows: Insert hook into 2 lps of ch, yo, pull through lp, shaping lp on hook to a small circle, bring clasp up, yo, pull through 2 lps on hook. Working in 2 lps of each ch, sc in each of next 15 (17, 19) ch, *sk 2 ch, 6 dc in next ch, sk 2 ch, sc in next ch*, rep from * to * 6 (7, 8) times, sc in each of rem ch, turn. [7 (8, 9) shells]

Row 2: Ch 1, working in bottom hump of beg ch, sc 2nd half of clasp into first ch as in row 1, sc into bottom of next ch 14 (16, 18) times, bsc in base of next sc, *sk next 2 ch, working in base of shell, work 6 dc, sk next 2 ch, bsc in base of next sc*, rep from * to * 6 (7, 8) times, sc into bottom hump of each rem ch, fasten off.

Wrap wire around clasp, then through several lps of closest st, rep once more, then wrap in and out through several strands of work. Cut and crimp tightly with small needle-nose pliers, making sure end does not poke out. Rep for opposite end.

Crossed-Cables Choker

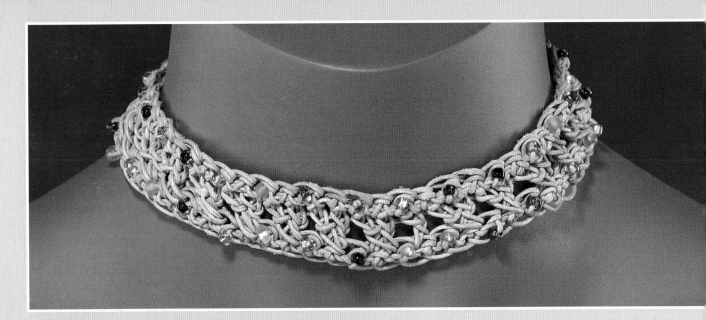

By Janet Rehfeldt

This retro-style choker is updated using either leather lacing or metallic thread and an easy-to-work crossed stitch that when worked in leather, wire, or hemp, looks like twisted cables. Long ties at the back allow you to adjust the choker to fit your neck or even use it as a belt in a pinch.

Skill Level: Easy ◼◼◻◻

Approximate Dimensions

Adjusts to fit most any neck circumference.

Featured Stitches

Bead single crochet (bsc), page 11
Chain (ch)
Crossed stitch, page 16
Single crochet (sc)

Materials

16 yds of one of the following:

1 mm round leather lacing from Tejas Lace, color 5053-04 Natural **2**

OR

Gatsby from Katia (77% viscose, 15% nylon, 8% metallic polyester; 129 yds; 50 g), color 20 **3**

OR

Hemp jewelry cord from Elements (100% hemp; 1-mm diameter; 40 yds; 36.5 m), color 1451 **2**

Size E-4 (3.5 mm) crochet hook (or size required to obtain gauge)

52 size 6/0 E beads

Charm or hanging bead (optional)

Craft or fabric glue if using Gatsby or hemp cord

Gauge

9 crossed sts = 4" using size E-4 (3.5 mm) crochet hook and leather or hemp

12 crossed sts = 4" using size E-4 (3.5 mm) crochet hook and Gatsby

> **NOTE:** *If you've never worked with leather, see "Crocheting with Leather" on page 8.*

Choker

String beads onto leather lacing (see page 10), or use a dab of craft or fabric glue smeared evenly along a 2" end of hemp or Gatsby, wiping off excess. Allow glue to dry, then use firm tip to string beads directly onto strand.

Row 1: Leaving an 18" tail, ch 57. Working in bottom hump of chain, sc in 2nd ch from hook, *bsc in next ch, sc in next ch*, rep from * to * across, turn. [56 sc]

Row 2: Ch 2, dc in first sc, *sk next sc, dc in next sc, dc in skipped sc*, rep from * to * to last sc, dc in last sc, turn. [27 crossed sts]

Row 3: Ch 1, sc in first dc, *bsc in next dc, sc in next dc*, rep from * to * across. Fasten off, leaving an 18" tail.

Attach an 18" length of lacing or ribbon to opposite end of choker at row 1, and a 2nd length at row 3 for ties. Thread 3 to 6 beads onto each end of ties and knot end of tie to keep beads in place. If desired, attach charm or hanging bead at center bottom of choker.

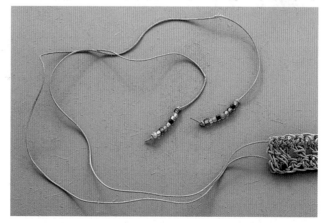

Magnetic Therapy Bracelet

By Janet Rehfeldt

Magnets have long been thought to have pain-relieving energy. Using varying sizes of magnetic hematite beads to form a vertical pattern gives an elegant style to this therapeutic bracelet.

Skill Level: Intermediate ◖■■■◗

Approximate Dimensions

5⅞ (7¼, 8½)" circumference

Featured Stitches

Bead single crochet (bsc), page 11
Chain (ch)
Double crochet (dc)
Single crochet (sc)
Slip stitch (sl st)

Materials

1 skein of Opera, size 5, from J&P Coats (100% cotton; 175 m; 50 g), color 501 or 561 🔟

Size A-1 (2 mm) crochet hook (or size required to obtain gauge)

2 (2, 2) large-swirl magnetic beads from Darice (5 x 11 mm), item 1965-78

14 (18, 22) medium, oval magnetic beads from Darice (4 x 7 mm), item 1965-77

24 (30, 36) small, round magnetic beads from Darice (4 mm), item 1965-75

1 small magnetic catch from Darice (⅜"), item 1968-49

Gauge

7.5 rows = 1" in sc using size A-1 (2 mm) crochet hook

Bracelet

> *NOTE: Bracelet is worked in rows from end to end. See page 11 for working with beads on the right and wrong sides of the work.*

String beads (see page 10) onto yarn as follows: 1 large, *3 small, 2 medium*, rep from * to * 6 (8, 10) times, 3 small, 1 large.

Row 1: Leaving a 6" tail, ch 4. Sc in 2nd ch from hook, sc in rem 2 ch, turn. [3 sc]

Row 2: Ch 1, sc in each sc, turn.

Row 3 (RS): Ch 1, sc in first sc, bring yarn to front of work, insert hook into next st, yo, bring up large bead, holding bead to front of work, yo and pull through 2 lps on hook, keeping bead to front of work, sc in last sc inserting hook under strand at left side edge of bead and into last st, turn.

Row 4 (WS): Ch 1, bsc 3 times, on last st, insert hook into last st and under strand from large bead on row 3, anchoring large bead to front of work.

Row 5: Ch 1, sc in each sc, turn.

Row 6: Ch 1, sc in first sc, (bsc, sc) in next st, sc in last st, turn.

Row 7: Ch 1, sc in first sc, sc between next 2 sc, sc in last sc, turn.

Row 8: Rep row 6.

Row 9: Rep row 7.

Row 10: Ch 1, bsc 3 times, turn.

Rep rows 5–10 another 6 (8, 10) times.

Next row: Ch 1, sc in first sc, bring yarn to front of work, insert hook into next st, yo, bring up large bead, holding bead to front of work, yo and pull through 2 lps on hook, keeping bead to front of work, sc in last sc.

Next row: Ch 1, sc in each sc, on last st, insert hook into last st and work around strand of large bead, anchoring large bead to front of work.

Next 2 rows: Ch 1, sc in each sc, turn. Do not fasten off.

Edging

With right side facing, ch 1, *sc in corner st, sc evenly along side edge, sc in corner, sl st in each sc on end*, rep from * to *. Fasten off, leaving a 6" tail. Using tails, sew clasp to each end. Weave in ends.

Felted Mini Purse

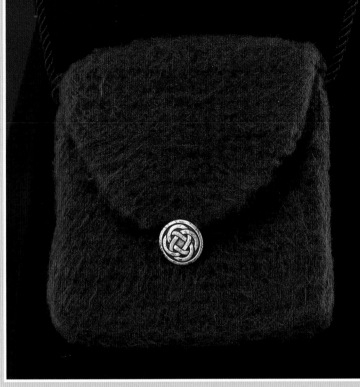

By Janet Rehfeldt

Be sophisticated or flirty with this Felted Mini Purse. Work up the purse without the eyelash yarn for a sophisticated look. The deep teal with multicolored metallic eyelash worked together on the flap makes for an elegant evening purse. Or if you're feeling a bit flirty, go for red with bright primary colors in a shorter version of eyelash yarn on the purse flap. Whatever you decide, this small felted purse is the ultimate accessory.

Skill Level: Easy ◼◼◻◻

Approximate Dimensions

Before felting: 9½" wide x 16½" high (including flap)

After felting: 5½" wide x 6" high with flap folded

Featured Stitches

Chain (ch)
Single crochet (sc)
Slip stitch (sl st)

Materials

1 ball of Nature Spun Worsted from Brown Sheep (100% wool; 245 yds/224 m; 3.5 oz/100 g) color N80 or N48 or N121 ◖4◗

Approx 15 yds of eyelash yarn (teal purse: Dazzlelash from Plymouth Yarn; 78% polyester, 22% rayon; 220 yds/201 m; 1.75 oz/50 g; color 107) (red purse: Plume FX from Berroco; 100% polyester; 63 yds; 20 g; color 6836) ◖2◗

Size H-8 (5 mm) crochet hook

Size L-9 (8 mm) crochet hook (or size required to obtain gauge)

36" to 45" braided or twisted cording or leather lacing for purse strap

1 button, ⅝" diameter

Small amount of heavy elastic thread

2 stitch markers

Gauge

8 sc = 4" using size L-9 (8 mm) hook before felting

Purse

Row 1: With larger hook, ch 20. Sc in 2nd ch from hook, sc in each ch, turn. [19 sc]

Row 2 (RS): Ch 1, sc in first sc, sc in each sc across, turn.

Rows 3–40: Rep row 2. Place a marker at each side edge on row 36.

Flap

Row 1 (dec row): Ch 1, sc in first sc, sc2tog, sc across to last 3 sts, sc2tog, sc in last sc, turn. [17 sc]

Rows 2–7: Rep row 1, turn. Fasten off. [5 sc at end of row 7]

Edging

Fold front of purse up to row 36 and pin in place. With smaller hook, attach yarn at one edge at row 36, loosely work 12 sl sts up side edge of flap, 5 sl sts across top edge, 12 sl sts down opposite edge of flap, 18 sl sts down side edge of purse, 2 sl sts in corner, 17 sl sts across bottom fold, 2 sl sts in opposite corner, 18 sl sts up remaining side edge. Sl st in same st as join, then sl st in each st across top front of purse. Fasten off and weave in ends.

Finishing

Felt as per instructions on page 12 and air-dry. It may take a few days for purse to completely dry.

Tie a knot at one end of cording for strap. About ¼" below top front edge, working from inside to outside of purse, pull unknotted end of cord through side edge of purse, using a small crochet hook. The knot will keep the cord in place on inside of purse. Rep for opposite side, working from outside to inside of purse and making sure cord is evenly placed. Knot end of cord on inside of purse.

Sew a button on front of purse. Using a small crochet hook, attach thick elastic thread to flap edge with a slip knot, make a chain that fits over the button plus 2 chains, turn, and sl st back along chain. Fasten off and sew opposite end of chain to purse at same place where elastic thread was joined. Weave in ends.

Beaded Amulet Bag

By Janet Rehfeldt

Skill Level: Easy ◖■◻◻

Approximate Dimensions

5¼" circumference at center of bag x 2½" tall (excluding edging)

Featured Stitches

Bead single crochet (bsc), page 11
Chain (ch)
Double crochet (dc)
Single crochet (sc)

Special Stitches

Small shell: 3 dc in same st

Large shell: 5 dc in same st

Ch 1 bead: Bring bead up to hook, yo, pull yarn through lp on hook (bead is secured in chain st).

Materials

1 skein of Opera, size 5, from J&P Coats (100% cotton; 175 m; 50 g), color 502, 560, or 558 ②

Size D-3 (3.35 mm) crochet hook (or size required to obtain gauge)

Size 5 (1.70 mm) steel crochet hook for optional crocheted strap

Approx 205 size E 6/0 beads for body of bag

Approx 32 size E 6/0 beads for beaded strap (optional)

Approx 80 size E 6/0 beads for beaded loops at bottom of bag (optional)

Rat-tail cording or small satin cording for strap and tie

Tassel (optional)

2 sets of toggle clasps for strap (optional)

Gauge

26 sc x 32 rows = 4" using size D-3 (3.35 mm) crochet hook

Bag

String beads onto thread (see page 10).

Rnd 1: With larger-size hook, ch 34. Sc in 2nd ch from hook, sc in each ch across. Being careful not to twist work, sl st to first sc to form a circle and close rnd. [33 sts]

Rnds 2–4: Sc in each sc.

Rnd 5: *Bsc in next st, sc in next st*, rep from * to * around.

Rnds 6–14: Rep rnd 5.

Rnds 15–20: Sc in each sc.

Lace Edging

Rnd 1 (eyelet rnd): *Sc, ch 1, sk 1 st*, rep from * to * to last sc, sc in last sc, sl st in first sc to close rnd. [16 ch spaces]

Rnd 2: Work 3 sc into each ch space, sk all sc, sl st in first sc to close rnd. [48 sc]

Rnd 3: Sl st in next sc, ch 2 (counts as 1 dc), 2 dc in same sl st, sk 2 sc, sc in next sc, *sk 2 sc, small shell in next sc, sk 2 sc, sc in next sc*, rep from * to * around, sl st in top of beg ch 2 to close rnd.

Rnd 4: Sc in next dc, large shell in next sc, sk 1 dc, sc in next dc (center of shell on previous rnd), *sk 1 dc, large shell in next sc, sk 1 dc, sc in next dc*, rep from * to * around, sl st in first sc to close rnd.

Rnd 5: Sc in same sl st as join, ch 5, sc in 3rd dc of large shell, *ch 5, sc in next sc, ch 5, sc in 3rd dc of large shell*, rep from * to * around, ch 5, sl st in first sc to close rnd.

Rnd 6: Ch 5, sl st in first ch-5 lp, ch 1 bead, sl st in same ch-5 lp, *ch 5, sl st in next ch-5 lp, ch 1 bead, sl st in same ch-5 lp*, rep from * to * around, ch 5, ch 1 bead, sl st in first ch-5 lp of rnd. Fasten off.

Finishing

Gather bottom of purse and pull tog. Run needle with thread back and forth through bottom to make sure it's tightly closed. Thread rat-tail cording or small satin cording through eyelet round to use as a pull tie or crochet a bead strap (directions below). Attach tassel to bottom of purse; or attach a large bead, then a tassel; or add looped beaded fringe (directions below).

Looped Beaded Fringe

Strand 80 beads onto thread, take 20 beads along thread, and fold up to form a lp, tack in place at bottom of bag, rep 3 times for 4 lps. Weave in all ends.

Crocheted Bead Strap

With a size 5 steel hook, leave a 6" tail, ch 193 (or a long chain of a multiple of 6 plus 1 to the length you want your strap). Working in bottom hump of ch, sl st in 2nd st from hook, sl st in next st, slip st with bead in next st (bring up a bead, insert hook into next st, yo, draw through stitch and lp on hook), *sl st in next 5 chains, sl st with bead in next st*, rep from * to * along ch, ending with a sl st in last 3 chains. Fasten off, leaving a 6" tail; sew strap to bag with tails or sew toggle clasps to strap and bag. Weave in ends.

Using toggle clasps to connect the strap to the bag allows you to change the strap to match your outfit. Use a crocheted bead strap (left) or silk cording (right).

Summer Mini Tote Bag

By Nancy Nehring

This little tote is perfect for summer errands. And every time you go outside, the white bag magically changes colors! UV-activated color-changing thread, beads, and a button do the trick. When your friends see this, they'll be so amazed, they'll want one too.

Skill Level: Easy ⬤⬤◻◻

Approximate Dimensions

13" wide x 3.5" deep x 10" tall, excluding handle

Featured Stitches

Back loop (bl)
Chain (ch)
Single crochet (sc)
Single crochet 2 together (sc2tog)

Special Stitch

Chain 2 mesh (see project instructions)

Materials

2 spools of crochet nylon from J&P Coats (100% nylon; 150 yds/137 m), color 1 ❸

2 spools of 560/4 color-changing serger thread from SolarActive (100% polypropylene; 90 yds/82 m), color blue ❶

Size 0 (2.55 mm) steel crochet hook

1 color-changing button from SolarActive, blue

90 color-changing pony beads from SolarActive, assorted colors

36"-long, ³⁄₁₆"-diameter vinyl clothesline for tubing

3" heavy wire, such as clothes-hanger wire, for top opening

3" x 7½" piece of plastic canvas for bag bottom

2 stitch markers

Gauge

20 sc x 20 rows = 4" using size 0 (2.55 mm) steel crochet hook

Bag

> NOTE: Work in oval without joining rounds, starting at bottom of bag and working upward.

Rnd 1: Using crochet nylon, ch 20. Working back along chain in bl, sc in 2nd ch from hook, sc in each of next 17 ch, 5 sc in last ch, working along other side of chain, sc in each of next 18 ch, 5 sc in last ch. Pm in st at each end. [46 sc]

Rnds 2 and 3: *Working through both lps of st, sc to 1 st before marker, 2 sc in next st, 3 sc in next st, 2 sc in next st, replace markers to mark end sts*, rep from * to * once. [62 sc]

Rnd 4: *Sc around to 2 sts before marker, 2 sc in next st, sc in next st, 2 sc in next st, sc in next st, 2 sc in next st, replace markers to mark end sts*, rep from * to * once. [68 sc]

Rnds 5–7: *Sc around to 3 sts before marker, 2 sc in next st, sc in next st, sc in next st, 2 sc in next st, sc in next st, sc in next st, 2 sc in next st, replace markers to mark end sts*, rep from * to * once. [84 sc]

Rnd 8: Sc in bl around.

Rnds 9–11: Sc through both lps around.

Rnd 12: Ch 1, *drop st from hook, put bead on hook, pick up dropped st and pull through bead, ch 1, sk 1 st, sc in next sc*, rep from * to * around.

Rnd 13: Add color-changing thread to crochet nylon and work the 2 threads tog as 1. *Ch 2, sc in sc of row below*, rep from * to * around, ending with sc over first ch 2.

Rnds 14–38: *Ch 2, sc over ch 2*, rep from * to * around.

Rnd 39: Cut and tie off color-changing thread. Cont to work with crochet nylon only. Ch 1, sc in next sc, *drop st from hook, put bead on hook, pick up dropped st and pull through bead, ch 1, sk 1 st, sc in next sc*, rep from * to * around, ending with sc in next sc.

Rnd 40: *Ch 2 over bead, sc in sc*, rep from * to * around.

Rnd 41: *Sc twice over ch 2, sc in sc*, rep from * to * around.

Rnds 42–44: Sc around.

Splice clothesline into circle by inserting one end of heavy wire into each hole in center of tubing ends and pushing until tubing meets. You'll have approx 132 sts around top opening. Divide so there are 23 sts each at center front and center back and 43 sts at each end. Adjust if you have more or fewer sts.

Rnd 45: *Sc over tubing and into edge of bag until you reach center 23 sts, work 2 more sc in last st, sc 85 over tubing only, sk 23 sts, work 3 sc in next st of bag edge*, rep from * to * once more until edge is complete.

Button Flap

At center back, attach crochet nylon 4 sts before center.

Rows 1–11: Ch 1, sc in next 9 sc of bag back, turn.

Row 12: Ch 1, sc in each of first 3 sc, ch 3, sc in last 3 sc, turn.

Rows 13–15: Ch 1, sc2tog, sc across to last 2 sts, sc2tog, turn.

Fasten off after row 15.

Finishing

Sew on button. Cut plastic canvas to shape of bag bottom. Sew into bottom of bag with crochet nylon and yarn needle.

Resources

The Beadery Craft Products
(401) 539-2432
www.thebeadery.com
Elements hemp jewelry cord

Berroco Inc.
(508) 278-2527
www.berroco.com
Glacé, Zodiac, Suede, Zen Colors, Optik, Plume FX, Mosaic FX, Mirror FX, Metallic FX, Chinchilla

Blue Sky Alpacas Inc.
(763) 753-5815
www.blueskyalpacas.com
100% alpaca

Brown Sheep Yarn Company
(308) 635-2198
www.brownsheep.com
Nature Spun worsted

The Caron Collection
(203) 381-9999
www.caron-net.com
Watercolours, Wildflowers

Cascade Yarns
(206) 574-0440
www.cascadeyarns.com
Fixation

Crystal Palace
(510) 237-9988
www.straw.com
Fizz, Waikiki

Dale of Norway
(800) 441-3253
www.dale.no
Dalegarn Baby Ull

Darice
(866) 432-7423
(440) 238-9150
www.darice.com
1-mm leather cord; 26-gauge craft wire; watch face; clasps; metal chain; 6/0 E beads

DMC
(973) 589-0606
www.dmc-usa.com
Cebilia; Senso Linen Cotton

Henry's Attic Inc.
(845) 783-3930
Fax: (845) 782-2548
16/4 Normandy Linen

J&P Coats
(864) 848-5610
www.coatsandclark.com
Opera 5, Crochet Nylon

Karabella Yarns
(800) 550-0898
www.karabellayarns.com
Lace Mohair

Knitting Fever Inc. and Euro Yarns
(516) 546-3600
www.knittingfever.com
Distributor for Schachenmayr Nomotta: Regia 4-ply, 6-color; Katia Gatsby, Sevilla; Sirdar Dune

Lacis
(510) 843-7178
www.lacis.com
Rayon bourdon gimp cording

Lion Brand Yarn Company
(800) 795-5466
www.lionbrand.com
Suede, Magic Stripes

Muench Yarns Inc.
(800) 733-9276
www.muenchyarns.com
Cleo Fabu

Plymouth Yarn Company Inc.
(215) 788-0459
www.plymouthyarn.com
Sockotta, Paradise, Eros, Eros Glitz, Alpaca DK, Dazzlelash

Skacel Collection, Inc.
PO Box 88110
Seattle, WA 98138-2110
(800) 255-1278
www.skacelknitting.com
Merino Lace

SolarActive International Inc.
(818) 996-8690
www.solaractiveintl.com
Color-changing serger thread, pony beads, and buttons

Tandy Leather Factory
(800) 687-0215
www.tandyleather.com
Tejas Lace 1-mm leather lacing; ⅛" flat leather lacing; ⅛" suede lacing

Trendsetter Yarns
(818) 780-5497
www.trendsetteryarns.com
Shadow; Metal; Binario; Eyelash

Meet the Designers

Without the help of my fellow designers, this book would not have had some of the truly great designs that it has. I am blessed with knowing and working with many of the most talented and truly wonderful designers in our industry. I would like to thank each and every one of them, not only for contributing to the book but also for considering me their friend.

Hazel Carter

Hazel was born in Cambridge, England. Her mother taught her to knit before she began school, then to crochet when she was six, so she has been doing both for more than 70 years. Having read English at Oxford University under such greats as C. S. Lewis and J. R. R. Tolkien, she switched to African languages and for some years taught at London University. Twenty-two years ago she came to the States to do likewise at the University of Wisconsin—Madison. Her publications include books and articles on various aspects of African languages and several forms of lace. Since retirement, she has parlayed the latter interest into a "second career" of producing knitting, crochet, tatting, and bobbin-lace designs. She lives in Madison, Wisconsin; her author-horsewoman daughter lives in Virginia with her husband and son, and Hazel's own artist son lives in London, England.

Darla J. Fanton

Darla, a needleworker for more than 20 years, has recently focused her talents on the double-ended and Tunisian crochet hooks. Through her innovative work in these techniques, she has breathed new life into crochet forms that had nearly disappeared from the scene. Her credits include magazine articles as well as leaflets by publishers such as ASN, Leisure Arts, Jeanette Crews, and her own pattern line, Designs by Darla J. She is a popular teacher at both national and regional conferences, such as Stitches, TNNA, and Fiber Arts Market. She is always delighted to share her special insight into crocheting with long hooks. Darla lives in the Portland, Oregon, area with her husband.

Karen Klemp

Karen is a retired U.S. Foreign Service officer, enjoying her second career as a crochet designer and teacher. She's been crocheting for more than 35 years and began designing garments years before she decided to publish any of her creations. Her designs have been featured in *Crochet Fantasy,* Crochet Guild of America patterns, *Quick & Easy Crochet,* and *Vogue Knitting.* She also has her own pattern line, Almost Amy. Karen was president of the Crochet Guild of America from 1999–2001 and served on the CGOA Board of Directors from 2001–2003. She teaches crochet locally and nationally and developed a crochet-instructor course for Capital Crocheters and Knitters, Inc. in Washington, DC. Karen lives in Arlington, Virginia, with her husband.

Carol Lykins

Carol has been knitting and crocheting since she was taught at an early age by her grandmother. Carol works with her sister, Janet Rehfeldt, and Knitted Threads Designs as a contract crocheter and pattern editor. They have codesigned many projects over the years, and although Carol enjoys staying in the background, she is quite a designer in her own right. Carol currently lives and does missionary work in Haiti with her husband.

Nancy Nehring

Nancy is a nationally recognized author, designer, and teacher in the needle-arts field. She is the author of several books, including *50 Heirloom Buttons to Make, The Lacy Knitting of Mary Schiffmann, Embellishing with Beads,* and *Teach Yourself Tunisian Crochet.* Numerous needle-art magazines, including *Threads, PieceWork,* and *Crochet!,* have carried her work. She has designed for DMC, Donna Karan, and Dynamic Resource Group, among others. Her Irish Crochet Doll Dress was awarded first place in crochet in the 2003 PieceWork Needleworker of the Year contest. She lectures and teaches locally, regionally, and nationally at Embroiderers' Guild of America

Seminar, Crochet Guild of America Chain Link, and Stitches. Nancy and her family live in Sunnyvale, California.

Kathleen Stuart

Kathleen Stuart learned to crochet when she was 10 and has been crocheting and designing crochet patterns ever since. Kathleen started her career in crochet in 1991 after reading about crochet designs and wanting to become a designer. She was amazed that her first design was accepted! She loves to crochet stuffed animals and toys along with afghans and other items. She especially enjoys using whimsy and color work in many of her designs. Her designs have been featured in publications by Martingale & Company, Dynamic Resource Group, Leisure Arts, Kustom Krafts, Fiber Circle Publishing, and Crafting Traditions. She is a professional member of the Crochet Guild of America and enjoys attending her local chapter, South Bay Crochet. Kathleen lives in San Jose, California, with her husband, Harold, and their four children.

Mary Jane Wood

Mary Jane learned to crochet from a McCall's *Learn to Crochet* magazine and has been crocheting nonstop for more than 30 years. Mary Jane's crochet designs have been featured in publications by Martingale & Company, Needlecraft Shop/Annie's Attic, and House of White Birches. She is the coauthor of *Crocheted Socks! 16 Fun-to-Stitch Patterns.* Since taking an early retirement from her job as a systems analyst, she has been an active participant in three different California Crochet Guild of America chapters. She developed and maintains a Web site for South Bay Crochet, one of the local crochet chapters. Mary Jane lives in San Francisco, California.

Acknowledgments

The following companies provided yarn for some of the projects in this book:

- Berroco Inc.
- Blue Sky Alpacas Inc.
- Brown Sheep Yarn Company
- Cascade Yarns
- Crystal Palace
- J&P Coats
- Knitting Fever Inc.
- Lion Brand Yarn Company
- Plymouth Yarn Company Inc.
- Skacel Collection, Inc.
- Tandy Leather Company
- The Caron Collection

The following shops were very generous with time and supplies:

- Susan's Fibers; Columbus, Wisconsin
- Prairie Junction; Sun Prairie, Wisconsin
- Amazing Yarns; Redwood City, California
- Knitting Bee; Portland, Oregon

Writing a book is an undertaking that boggles the mind when you think of the number of people and resources that are involved. If it were not for all the help and encouragement that I received from the wonderful staff at Martingale, not only could I have possibly gone insane, but this project would never have been able to evolve into the professional and creative work that it has become.

There are several people to whom I owe a great deal and I will never be able to thank them enough for their help and contributions.

Karen Soltys; Acquisitions and Development Editor: Thank you so much for seeing that a book on upscale crocheted accessories was a subject well worth exploring. Without your help, this book would not have been accomplished.

Terry Martin; author liaison: You're always so calm and encouraging in seeing me through every detail and smoothing out every wrinkle whenever we work together.

Donna Druchunas; technical editor: Donna, you are a wizard! Thank you for grooming my work and making it all come together.

Timothy Maher and Laurel Strand; illustrators: Tim, thank you so much for creating any and all illustrations I ever ask for. As always, you are extremely patient with the short deadlines I throw at you. Laurel, thank you for your dedication to quality and for working so hard to make sure every illustration is clear and accurate.

Carol Lykins; sister, friend, and confidant: I can never thank you enough for all you do and you are always there for me, crocheting through all hours of the day and night to get models finished for me.

Sandy Jones: Thank you so much for coming to my aid and helping me to organize and get it all together.

Nancy Nehring: You are truly an inspiration in your talents and advice. Thank you for being there.

Lois Blanchard: Thank you for coming in at the eleventh hour. Your help and suggestions were invaluable. I love that your favorite pattern is the Pull-Up Pinkies.

Meet the Author

Janet Rehfeldt has been knitting and crocheting since the age of seven. She is the owner of Knitted Threads Designs and also an author, instructor, and designer. Her designs can be found in leading knitting and crochet magazines, including *Crochet Fantasy, Crochet!,* and *Machine Knitters Source.* Her designs also appear in publications by House of White Birches, the Needlecraft Shop/Annie's Attic, Plymouth Yarns, and Skacel Collections, Inc. She coauthored *Crocheted Socks! 16 Fun-to-Stitch Patterns* (Martingale & Company, 2003). She teaches on both a local and national-level. Her Web site (www.knittedthreads.com) offers information, tips, and techniques for crocheters, hand knitters, and machine knitters. Janet lives in Sun Prairie, Wisconsin, with her husband, their golden retriever, and two cats.